With Purpose On Purpose

The Poetry and Reflections
of
Sasha E. Medina

ISBN:1482736128
ISBN-13: 978-1482736120

iii

Dedication

I dedicate this book first and foremost to my Lord and Savior Jesus Christ. All my inspiration comes directly from God and so I give all credit to Him. I'd also like to dedicate this book to my family who has always been so supportive of my writing and has always pushed me to continue fulfilling God's purpose for my life. You've encouraged me and motivated me more than you could ever know and for that I thank you.

I also dedicate this book just as much to all of my friends and family in Christ who have supported my writing throughout the years and have been waiting for this book to come out. Finally, I dedicate it to you, reader who picked up my book. I pray that the words within this book will be a blessing and have an impact on your life.

Thank you for your support in purchasing this book.

-Sasha E. Medina

Contents

Acknowledgments

I would like to thank my brother Xavier. Without you this wouldn't be possible. You truly are the glue that holds me together even if you don't know it. Thanks for the countless hours you've spent listening to my poems. I will forever cherish those moments. I love you very much. Thank you for being my brother.

Introduction

So, With Purpose On Purpose...What does that mean? Well let's start from the beginning. It all starts with God. God is the creator of all things. He is the creator of the universe, the creator of time, the creator of all living things and ultimately the creator of you and I. Now, when God creates something, He creates it with a purpose. There are no coincidences in God (Proverbs 16:4; 19:21). Once He decides to do something there is no changing His mind; He is unchangeable (Psalm 102:25-27). So if God is your creator and He creates things with a purpose then that means that you were created with a purpose and God isn't going to change His mind about you or the purpose He created you for.

So the purpose of this book is to motivate you and empower you to find and fulfill the purpose for which God created you. The bible says that we were created in the image and likeness of God. That means we were created to be like God. We are supposed to reflect His personality and His ways. So, if God does everything on purpose and with a purpose and we are to be like our father, then we too must do things on purpose and with a purpose. If each and every one of us has a purpose then we must live our lives intentionally trying to fulfill it; the intentional fulfillment of our purpose is what this book's title refers to. Every single day we are given is a gift from God and another opportunity to move one step closer to fulfilling the plans that He has for our lives.

The bible recounts the story of a man named Jonah. God's will for Him was that he would go to the city of Nineveh and evangelize and tell the people of that city to repent of their sins. Jonah didn't want to do this so instead he ran off on a boat to the city of Tarshish. But on the way to Tarshish, God sent a violent

1

storm on the sea and Jonah confessed that the he (Jonah) was the cause of the storm. The crew threw Jonah overboard and he was swallowed by a big fish. Immediately the storm ceased. Jonah remained in the belly of the fish for three days and when God finally let him out, he went to Nineveh and spoke to the people and they repented and were saved from destruction.

So what's the moral of the story? Jonah spent three days in the belly of a fish; three days in which he was sitting in darkness and unable to go anywhere. Sometimes we find ourselves in a metaphorical belly of a fish; in a place of darkness, emptiness and immobility. We find ourselves in this place at times in our lives when we are searching for meaning and seeking a purpose to our existence. We try to fulfill our emptiness with so many things; people, achievements, recognition, all of which are temporary fixes. Yet, none of these things fully satisfy us. The inner most depths of our souls seek something more. Could it be that the created (you and I) do in fact need a relationship with the Creator? That is for you to answer.

Nevertheless, the belly of the fish was not made for you. It is a temporary state, a passing season on the way to fulfilling God's purpose for your life. Don't waste anymore time in this season. Don't waste anymore time in your life! Wherever your purpose is, there you will find prosperity and satisfaction. So don't prolong the process. Seek a relationship with God, seek His purpose, work to fulfill it, and you will find satisfaction, fulfillment and joy in your life.

So if you didn't know that your life had a purpose, it does. I pray that this book will motivate you to seek out that purpose and live your life intentionally trying to fulfill it. Be blessed!

-1-

Speak. Empower. Motivate.

The poems in this chapter are empowerment poems. Their intention is to speak to your mind, empower your life, and motivate you. Too often, I think we as human beings lose our motivation and drive in life as we face day to day challenges. At times we forget that we have a purpose, that we are children of God, and that the Word of God tells us that no weapon formed against us can prosper (Isaiah 54:17). Sometimes we just need to be reminded that we are more than conquerors in Christ who loved us (Romans 8:37). So these poems are for those days when you need to remind yourself of who you are in Christ.

The Silent Poet

If I do not speak, then I am weak. If I do not say what's on my mind, then I will be forgotten and left behind.

If the words God has placed in my head are never said, I might as well be dead.

If I never preach of His goodness and mercy, what good will that be?

If I don't respond to His calling and fulfill my purpose, then there is no truth in me.

If I don't speak, if I don't testify, if I'm too ashamed to let Him be glorified, then what's the purpose of life?

If God placed His words in my mouth, and I choose never to speak out, then my life is meaningless.

Unless…
Unless I speak. Unless I let His words flow through me, letting Him take control totally and completely, uncensored and not even a bit discreetly, I have to let Him be.

 For it's His purpose that His words be heard. So I don't need to be nervous, scared or deterred. If it's my Father that I represent on this earth, then no weapon formed against me can prosper. I can't be stirred, pushed over to the side or deferred, for it's His word beating inside my heart like a caged bird. So I've got to let it out, I can't hold it much longer, every second that passes I hear His voice getting stronger.

So, no I can't be quiet, no I won't be silent! If I don't speak of my God's praises then the stones will make a riot, and I refuse to let some rocks take my opportunity to be shining. See it's MY purpose to praise Him, that's the reason that I'm writing, and it's His perfect timing. So my mind isn't minding those who think it's necessary to remind me that time's not rewinding. But I'm not wasting time, see it's my purpose I'm unwinding. For if I don't speak now I can't forever hold my peace, because an internal battle is what'll consequently unleash. So don't hush me please, don't you dare try to stop me, because I will keep proclaiming my King, until my heart starts to drop beats...

Causing me to slow down, relax and take it easy. Because it's not the world that I'm pleasing, it's your conscience I'm appeasing; easing in, squeezing, and making room for the real King. True worship is what He's seeking, so don't waste time looking at me. It's Him you should be seeing. It's Him that I'm revealing, His words that I'm repeating. It's Him who does the healing, reaching to your inner feelings, peeling back what you're concealing, so that your life can have new meaning.

See it's time we start believing. It's time we start receiving. I'm not speaking words void of meaning. Forget a rhyme if it's intervening with the message that I'm bringing. Jesus died to save you, that's what it comes down to. He loved you so much when He didn't even have to. You with all your flaws, all your mistakes and all your sinning. He could've stayed in heaven and let us all be condemned but thank God for His mercy, He gave us a new beginning. That means you're a new creation, your past doesn't have to define you. See the reason I speak these words today is because God wanted them to find you. There are no coincidences in God, that's why I can't be quiet, that's why these words I have to speak, that's why I just can't fight it.

For God so loved the world... that's the reason I'm not silent.

Empowered State of Mind

This is a message to my generation. It seems we're falling into condemnation, subtly but surely losing our concentration, losing our determination to seek God and witness His manifestation in our lives. Too busy with our infatuation with TV, video games, and the garbage coming out of popular radio stations. See no one realizes that the worst influences don't come from being under the influence but rather by being influenced by people of influence. Don't you realize that what you let your ears listen to can stop you from letting God come through? Youth I speak to you! Galatians 5:7-8 "who hindered you from obeying the truth? This influence doesn't come from Him who calls you". So I ask you, what's influencing you? See I see too many Jay-Z fans these days, regardless of the fact that he's made the multitudes repeat that "Jesus can't save". But I won't even try to compete with those who claim, "You have to understand the context of what he was saying". Saying is what I'm doing, and I'm doing what God's saying. Don't you realize that anything you're defending before God becomes the god that you're praising?

And while I lack the "Empire State of Mind", I have an empowered state of mind. Because I will empower this generation until God tells me it's my time. So don't tell me that it's impossible because that's the enemy's biggest lie! Don't tell me the world's too big to reach out to, when the bible tells me that it's my Father's foot stool in Matthew 5:35! Don't tell me I'm going to run out of time when I serve the Alpha and Omega who exists outside of time! He's the beginning and the end. Principio y fin. No, I'm not leaving this place without exalting my King. Without exalting the one who gave His life for me because if I'm standing here today it's not for you to see me. So God make me invisible so it's you that they see, because if not there's no purpose in the words that I speak…

Empower, motivate, that's what He called me to do. So I'm going to keep speaking these words until my face turns blue. Blue, the color of the sky that God finished creating along with the earth in Genesis 2. Genesis 2, also the chapter where my kind was created. You know, the suitable helper that would help man follow God's plans through. So women don't you ever let a man devalue you. Don't ever think you're worthless when God made you with purpose.

You were predestined for greatness. Youth it's time to wake up! Laziness is just the enemy's strategy to try to disrupt the purpose God gave you; the reason He made you. If you don't start fighting for that purpose then you've already given up. See the enemy knows just how to corrupt. He knows how to tempt you to self-destruct. He knows you have a purpose that he must interrupt because if not it's his head that your foot will crush. So don't you be intimidated, don't you give up! Because the Creator of the universe is the one who lifts you up. So if a thousand times you fall, then a thousand times you get up! Because I can guarantee you that God will never give up.

So I refuse to believe the enemy's lies, when he tells me I'm only saying pointless rhymes, that my words won't reach lives, and that I'm wasting my time. Because although I'm not perfect, the One who's in me is. He filled me with purpose so I could tell the world that He lives, that He died and resurrected to save you and cleanse you of sin. The I Am that I Am, He still is what He is, and He did what He did, so that through us He could live. He's perfecting His love, perfecting His purpose. It's you He predestined, it's you that He's chosen. So today you stop believing that your life is worthless. Today you start declaring "I have a purpose!" Today you start behaving like you're a different person, and today you start living your life knowing that you've been chosen!

I Will Not Be Moved

I'm tired of listening to what the world has to say about me. Quite frankly, I find it illogical to heed the words of those who doubt me; of those who don't realize what the world would be without me. Unknowingly they criticize me, shouting, and attempting to demoralize me, antagonize me, take away my strength, and anesthetize me. But little do they know

I will not be moved.

But the world pushes and shoves, it uses every trick in the book it can get a hold of. It tempts me with the fornicated version of love that doesn't fill me up but instead falls short of the glory of God. For the world is not admitting of its flaws. Disguised in sheep's clothing, it hides well its claws. It entices and draws with its applause but though empty fame might leave in awe, the line between life and death is clearly drawn. So I do not follow ways of men, I walk in the direction of divine law. So if your intention was to see me fall, to keep running towards me and give me your all, then I suggest you take a minute, I suggest you take a pause. Because against all the odds

I will not be moved.

Now you can try to scare me, tempt me, dare me, offer all the world has to share with me, compare the world's gifts with those of the heavenly. You can show me the fake version of Christianity, and tell me it's ok to sin and then say the Lord 's Prayer with me, but I tell you beware of me. For I come with a Word declared in me, and I will not be impaired, by evil looks and stares, by words of ignorance and glares, so be prepared,

For, I will not be moved.

I will not be pushed over to the side. I will not be silenced or denied the right to speak the truth inside. For though in weakness you may push me down, in strength I will arise. His word will be my guide. My body is His temple in which sin shall not reside. And He shall not be set aside. In Him I set my sight, in Him I will confide and lay down my pride. For the humble He shall rise. For His purposes I lay my life, to be a living sacrifice. No more tears will I cry for I stand in His might. So try to push me if only one time, so that you may witness with your own eyes

That I will not be moved.

Enough

I feel so afraid. These fears are closing in on me. All of my worst nightmares are trying to creep up on me. Loneliness. Lack of acceptance. Low self-esteem. I'm not going to make it. Goals too high to reach. Everyone else is better than me. I don't want to let go of what I have left. I'm wasting my time. I won't amount to anything in life. No one will ever love me. I'll never have a happy ending! I'm too shy to say what's on my mind. Who cares what I have to say? Who wants to listen to me anyway as I cry these tears away?

Wait, wait, wait! That's about enough... I said enough! Enough with these fears! Enough with all the tears! Enough with the shying away and trying to disappear! My time isn't close by, my time isn't near. My time is right now! My time is right here! I fulfill my resolutions today! I'm not waiting until New Years! Enough of the waiting! The road has been cleared! The light has turned green and I'm going full gear! Enough with the low self-esteem, I see a princess in the mirror! And loneliness? What's with that? Last time I checked my God is with me EVERYWHERE! And if the ignorant don't want to listen then I say who cares? I'm talking to those who want to be blessed when they hear. The good news is flowing from my lips and I'm ready to declare, Jesus died on the cross to give you salvation, freedom, power, self-control and love, not for you to have a spirit of fear.

So listen here, because I'm going to speak, empower, and motivate until these walls of fear I tear down. Until all these tears I let out. Until this world is cured of the insanity that it breeds around. Until you realize that you are blessed without any doubt. That you will make it and to greatness is what you'll amount. There's no time to waste, your time is right now! God is calling you out. But He can only use you, as much as you allow…

Dying

Why do we live as if we can't die? Wasting precious time, poisoning people's minds, telling pointless lies, selling worthless rhymes, living useless lives, but failing to realize that every day we live is one day closer to the day we die. Do we not value life? Or has our mentality simply been minimized to conversations about who has more swag or who dresses more fly? And I'm not trying to offend anyone with the message I imply, but my concern is not to make you feel good but to open up your eyes.

You see, too many times, I've seen people die with unfulfilled dreams and unsatisfied lives because they didn't know the day they would die. And waking up on that last morning they didn't realize that day would be the end of the line. There was no chance to say goodbye. There were no last few words before they died and no great stories told about their lives. But they left one thing behind; memories attached to names, attached to faces, attached to minds. Each with a mind that lived on even as the body died.

A mind we all have but don't put to good use most at times. A mind filled with goals and dreams but no action to pursue them. But I'm tired of seeing so much wasted potential. It's so sad to see that "someday" is the word that's most influential. They fail to see that their decisions of today are consequential. For they have yet to accept He that is truly essential; the God who sees it all, even what they thought was confidential.

And so in their minds they think that from death they can hide; that they don't need God to survive. They fail to recognize that one day they'll die, and that when that day arrives, nothing else on earth can guarantee eternal life. But they push this thought to the side because it doesn't really fit in with their plan for life. They fool themselves thinking "tonight isn't my night". Entertaining the thought that they're in control of their life. But we don't choose to be born, just like we don't choose to die. For just as God has given you life, He can take it back in the blink of an eye. So meditate on these lines, and let them sink in to your minds. Because our existence is only a spec in time and we only get one chance to live out this life. So will you ride or die for Christ and fulfill His purpose in your life? Or will you ride your way through life, aimless heading straight for your demise?

Look At Me

Look at me,

What do you see?

Is it the color of my eyes? The thickness of my thighs? Whether my hips are narrow or wide, my legs short and stocky or thin, tall and defined? Is it the color that my hair is dyed? The make-up that hides the tears that yesterday I cried? Or do you see the radiance that from inside me shines? The pride with which I carry myself and hold my head up high? Because I recognize the treasure placed in me by the Most High.

Look at me again,

Closely this time.

Do I look like those flawless, wanna-be goddess, dressed to impress, gotta show a little more flesh, just to get some respect, females that are portrayed in magazines, only after hours of make-up and editing? Perfection. That's what we aim for. But corruption is what we pay for when tears are shed behind closed doors. Fake personalities we seem to beg for. The real woman is ignored, her outer beauty's what's adored, while her body she abhors. We're spending countless dollars, on make-up, surgeries, anti-aging creams and more.

We're trying to cover up flaws almost as if "you made a mistake!" is what we try to tell God. And in return we become frauds, recognizing the outer for beauty while the inner fills itself with hideous impurity. Our faces become our security; these masks we dare not take off. It's a lack of maturity, of not knowing better than to think that God doesn't see past our outer physique. Like Adam and Eve we fail to take accountability when we realize God sees us in our intimate nudity, where shame lies for lack of responsibility.

So again I say look at me

Because I haven't been perfected. Look at me because I'm flawed and I'm defected. Look at me closely, because I've lost my fear of being neglected. Because I walk over the ashes of rejection. Look at me because I've learned to fly above the negativity the media has projected. Look at me because my beauty comes from where you least expect it. My beauty only shines because I am His reflection, the One who died and resurrected, so that one day I could reach redemption.

Look at me,

But close your eyes

And listen to my voice for it wears no disguise. Close your eyes if only this time. Because my outer appearance doesn't represent me but rather it is the vessel that withholds me and prevents me from taking off this mask that protects me. See, I understand now why the blind are more free, because they see humanity through the words that we speak. Through the sounds that the heart lets slip through our lips. They see humanity the way that God sees.

So one last time,

Just look at me.

And tell me now, what do you see?

I Refuse

I REFUSE

To bow down before the problems that surround me. Never will I surrender to the negativity around me. Call me optimistic but pessimism won't confound me. I can rejoice now everyday because tears can never drown me.

I REFUSE

To see myself cry, over mistakes, regrets, or any guy. I pray that I will never deny the falls I make because from them I arise. Let me not forget that beneath my arms are wings to fly. And that the sky is not my limit so I must fly high. Higher than the reach of my eyes, the rules of gravity I will defy. I'm as light as a feather regardless of what people may see on the outside. Because I REFUSE to define my worth by the thickness of my thighs. I WILL hold my head up high. Can anyone judge me? Let them try! Because regardless of what anyone says, I maintain my pride. Let it be known that I'm not afraid to shine. And that no matter who gets in my way I will survive.

Because I REFUSE

To become another statistic. I refuse to be "that girl". To be another number in this world. Because more than cuteness hides behind my curls. Empowering thoughts that form powerful words. And I know I'll be heard, because people are desperate to learn. And I'm done with the absurd, with the stereotypes that are constantly spurred, with the lies that my vision have blurred. Enough has occurred, enough I have heard! I'm too smart to be deterred! So call me a nerd, or a geek if that's what you'd prefer because I will not cease my written words until I know this world is cured.

And I REFUSE

To be used, to be silenced or abused because I will not be reduced to the five feet that stretch between my head and my shoes. Height will never be my excuse, because from this small body comes a big point of view. Not always at the right angle because I see things obtuse. I see people past their hues and into their minds I induce words that are so deep I could be a muse. Because what I have to say is bound to reproduce. And so no one who tries will ever leave a bruise. And no matter what threats or fear they try to produce, silence from my lips is just something I REFUSE.

If Tomorrow

If tomorrow, tomorrow, they should tell you I've died, have no sorrow, no sorrow, for they have told you bad lies. For though my body they have taken, my soul is still alive. I have only moved to the palace with my Father in the sky. His kingdom is so beautiful, but He says it's also mine, so don't be sad and do not cry because I didn't say goodbye. For I will see you again when you are finally alive.

When you get to see the ocean here, it's so crystallized and clear that all of my defects in its reflection disappear. And the streets, they do glimmer as the angels do cheer, "he's here, he's here! he's finally here!" And everyone is happy and there is no fear. The only thing missing is you right here, but Eternal Father says, "one day you'll be near".

So if they've told you that I've passed away, tell them they're ridiculous and that I'm more than okay. That I am in glory only a prayer away and that I am with my Father in His perfect place.

But if they tell you that I suffered, that I will never breathe again, that I am gone, that there's no hope or that in days I will be dead, tell them that death is for the weak but King's choose life instead. I have worn my robe, my crown's placed on my head. Tell them my name was in His book and He has always called me friend.

So if tomorrow, tomorrow, they should say that I've died, then have no sorrow, no sorrow for I've never been more alive.

-2-

A Woman's Worth

The poems in this section are mostly for women. Some are empowering, some are sad, some are just experiences that we have as women. I fear that too many of us women have been influenced by society and the media to try to be physically perfect. But this obsession with image has stunted many of us spiritually. Low self-esteem is an epidemic that is attacking women all over the United States. Low self-esteem has taken over because women are looking at themselves through the mirror of society instead of looking at themselves through the eyes of God. We were created in the image and likeness of God. We should not be allowing society or the media to define who we are, but rather we should be letting God define us and we should secure our identity in Him. For, if we don't know our self worth, if we don't know who we are or what our true identity is, then we will never be able to see what our purpose is. I hope these poems will empower you women. I pray that you will begin to see yourselves the way that God sees you and that you decide to raise your standards and start behaving like the daughters of God that you were always predestined to be.

My Daughter, Love Me First

Dear Daughter,

I know you've been asking yourself why love is so hard, why it hurts so much and why you always seem to end up with a broken heart. Why it is people hurt you without seeming to care, without seeming to notice that you give your all from the start. I know you've loved many times and many times you've been scarred. But I'm here to offer you a new beginning, I'm here to offer you a new start. But first you must answer a question, are you willing to let me guard your heart?

Are you willing to give your love to me the way you've given it to those men who hurt you? Because hurt you is something I won't do. I can promise that I will never abandon or desert you. I still see you as pure in my eyes even though those men have tried to pervert you. They've tried to get you to revert into a woman who doesn't care, who claims that love doesn't really concern you, when you know love is the thing you've searched for most. It's the thing you felt would make you complete, and make everything else feel like it could finally come to a close.

And although you're right, you've looked for that love in all the wrong places. Because the only love that can make you complete is speaking to you from the place where grace is. Imagine that I'm looking at you face to face and your heart starts beating at a faster pace, nothing else matters, everything else around you is erased, and now I tell you that I love you...

But it seems like it's still not enough for you. See I can say in all honesty that I love you more than life because I actually gave my life for you; I paid the ultimate price. You ask me why love hurts. I'll explain it one more time. When I got on that cross, tears for you I did cry. And although I knew you'd be unfaithful to me, that you'd sin, cheat and lie, I still got on that cross just so you could be mine. I made the decision to die, not because you deserved it but because I loved you more than life. Because I was willing to go through pain and suffering just to have you by my side. And some days you still reject me, some days you still neglect to realize that my love for you is deeper than the love any man can provide. That if you gave me your heart first I would guard it with my life and only give it to the man who truly deserves all the love you have to offer inside. A man who wouldn't make you cry, who loves me too, so he'll know how to love you.

He'll know how to treat you like a queen, because he'll have a relationship with me. And he'll know how much I love you so he won't dare to hurt your feelings. I have that man for you but first I want to be that man for you. The one who won't hurt you, who will never desert you, who would never even think of leaving you alone in your time of need. Don't you realize that the meaning of the word love is Me and that without Me it's impossible to find the real thing? You'll only find hollow "I love you's" attached to strings and bed springs. But the man who truly loves you won't think about those things. He'll respect you for your heart and mind before he notices your body. But I need you to trust me with your heart, to simply believe in me. Don't you know you're so special to me and that I want you to be with me in this life and for all eternity? I'll give you the desires of your heart but I need you to seek me. I know you've been hurt by what men call love but I'm here to show you the real thing. So are you ready for true love or will you settle for the next best thing? I've always been there waiting for you and I continue to wait patiently. But I want to be able to make you happy now and you just keep stalling me. I'm reaching out to you again. So this time, will you call on me? Sincerely, Jesus Christ aka Love (the real thing)

Reclaiming Woman's True Identity

Today I take a stand, I take an oath, I make a promise, to be the best woman that I can, dignified, untainted, and honest. I will be what God defines me as, instead of a product of my past. So I hold fast to what God says about me, forgetting what the world thinks I should be. See, God already predetermined what I would be. So I take a stand for every girl, and for every woman feeling misunderstood. See, it's time that we finally became free: free from every person who stole time from our dreams, free from every person who took advantage of our personalities and mistook our sweetness for weakness, free from every person who told us we wouldn't amount to anything, free from every person who took a piece of us and never gave it back, free from every label that was given to us making us feel that somehow we lacked, purity or the chance to be forgiven by a God who's too holy to be associated with our mess. But guess what?

Today that all comes to an end. Today is the day to reclaim ourselves and become whole again. Today is a day for redemption, and to allow God to cleanse, to heal our wounds and begin to mend, every emotional ache, every heart break. It's time to let God erase our past mistakes, take away the yoke of our pain, and remove the burden of the guilt that we carry every day. It's time to finally let Him in and let Him have His way. It's time to reclaim all the respect and dignity that the world tried to strip away. It's time to take back our bodies from those who with sweet words stole our crowns and put us to shame. It's time to regain our purity, to become women with purpose ready to raise our standards and our priorities. It's time we put God first and with our lives glorify His name. It's time we realize that we are capable of change: that we are not forever cursed, that we've been immersed in His mercy, and His love has the power to reverse, all our mistakes and all our past failures. See, only He can quench our thirst, only He can fill that emptiness and that lack of love that brought us to our worst. Our identities have been dispersed among all those who nursed our weaknesses when we were hurt; when we thought no one would love us. They coerced us with their words. But it's time we let our Father remind us of who we really were.

And so. I'm reclaiming my body, I'm reclaiming myself, because I refuse to look at myself through the eyes of someone else! Or through the eyes of a man who can't seem to understand, that God's purpose and plan for me, wasn't to wait on a man's foot and hand. It wasn't to be the one night stand. It wasn't to be an object that he could drop and pick back up at his demand. But in fact God's plan was so grand, His love so immense, His thought process so intricate and intense, that He saw it wasn't good for man to be alone and hence from his rib He extracted the best friend. The one who would be the suitable helper, the bone of his bone, the flesh of his flesh, the one on whom he could depend, both remaining faithful to the end. See women, we weren't made to be shamed. We weren't made to be depressed. We were made to be one, carrying out God's purpose and we can't afford to waste time with anyone who will deter it.

So, know that when bad relationships fail it's because God only wants what's best. Our hearts He yearns to protect. He will not abandon us in our mess. See, that's not in His best interest. We are His loved daughters, our Daddy we must represent. He loves us more than we can imagine. His love in us He must perfect. We deserve to be loved, protected, and cherished. It was never His intention for us to have to deal with heart ache, disillusion and disparage. His intention was for man and woman to become one in marriage and to fulfill His purpose is our inheritance.

We no longer have to live in the shadows of our pasts. We are new creations worth much more than precious stones. So, we must protect our bodies. Our temple is our home; dwelling place of the holy ghost. It's time we place our crowns of dignity back on our heads and reclaim our access to the throne. It's time we start behaving like the queens we were meant to be and make our values known. We weren't made to be disowned, weren't made to cry tears, weren't made to feel alone, having a self-esteem that's low. We deserve better, we can be better. God needs us to raise our standards and make it well known that we are daughters of the Most High and we won't accept anything below. So ladies, take care of your hearts, guard your bodies and your souls, and cherish the words that God in your spirit has sown. For though you were taken from man's bone, it's God's spirit that your temple holds. So treat yourselves with respect and always know, that the God who is with you will never ever leave you alone.

Me and Her

She lies in bed with me at night.

She pushes me to fight.

She's the fire that ignites

And inspires me to write.

She says everything will be alright

And from the mirror looks into my eyes.

She's intense, but beautiful in every sense.

Wise beyond her years, her knowledge of me is dense.

And the secrets she carries are the cause of my suspense.

So many things I want to ask, so many things left to discuss.

But time stands between us like a mask,

To bring our voices to a hush.

But when time ticks towards destiny,

I know that she and I will finally meet.

For we are one person, her and me;

The woman that I am, and the one I'm meant to be.

Nine

Age eighteen.

Senior year already. I've grown into this body, and now they seem to notice me. In fact they all know me. I go to every party, I smoke and I drink. I do the same thing as every other average teen. And all the boys like me, promiscuity could it be? Maybe, but who cares as long as I get the attention I need. As long as I don't have to go home, I'll seduce anybody. I'd rather be on the streets than return to that *thing*. They call it a home but it reeks of a disgusting memory I dare not speak. But I'm the party girl who everyone wants to be around. Girls envy me and wish they were me, because they know prom queen I'll be crowned. But these girls have no idea of the injustices this world revolves around. They wouldn't last two days walking on my same ground. And these guys, they fall at my feet; they think I'm their dream girl. But little do they know that I use them to drown, that I die a little more inside every time I get around. They take me as their little prize, not knowing the dirty secret I hold inside. But it serves them right, because all men are alike. And when I kiss them, I never close my eyes because that's when they'll strike. And if they ever say "I love you", then it's time to take a hike because like I said before, ALL men are alike.

Age fifteen.

No one even looks at me. No one sees past my flat chest and these braces in my teeth. No one seems to know the me that is beneath; the me with no self-esteem. It's like I wear a cloak of invisibility, ever since HE...(sigh) I must not speak of those things. I go through life as a puppet, don't know who pulls my strings, but I know it's not me. My teachers say I'm smart, that I can do better than C's and D's, that I should socialize with others and let them get to know me. If only they knew...

Age twelve.

No one seems to know I'm going through hell and that I'm shaking with terror of that dismissal bell. I don't want to go home and hear HIM yell. I wonder if anyone senses that smell. No. They couldn't, I hide it well. Parent teacher conferences. A good image HE must sell. Wouldn't want anyone to know that HE's the Devil, and we live in hell. "Your father's doing well with business" they say, "you must be very proud". "Oh yes, he's so renowned", I say. I figure why not play into the cynicism as well and let the irony make him drown. HE makes these faces of disapproval at me but I don't care who's around. I can't wait for the day when his secret is found. Maybe then will I return to life and be unburied from the ground. Maybe then will I be sound.

Age nine.

Daddy says he's got a surprise. He comes in my room and locks the door behind. Tells me to close my eyes and not to worry, that it'll be fine. But when I opened them, what I saw sent a chill up my spine. And daddy touched me in places I wanna erase from my mind. And he made these faces that made me wish I could die. This wasn't much of a surprise and no one heard my screams and cries! And daddy said it was a secret just between him and I, that no one should know, that they'd think it was a lie. He said, "wipe those tears from your eyes before your mom comes home asking why". So I tried and I tried, but my stupid eyes, they wouldn't stop building up these tears and my disgusting body wouldn't stop shaking in fear. And I just wanna disappear but I keep looking in the mirror, and I'm still here...

I'm still here.

Reflection: "Nine"

This poem is not based on a true story. However, I realize that there are many women who have been sexually molested or physically abused in their homes. Such situations cause women to have low self-esteem, to feel as if they are nothing, and many times, to feel that they have brought the harm upon themselves. Like the female in this poem, many females try to hide the scars of the abuse. If you fit into any of these categories, there's something I want you to know. God has not abandoned you. He has seen every tear you have cried, and it hurts Him to know that you had to deal with all the pain that came with it.

Nevertheless, the bible says in Isaiah 53:4 "Surely He [Jesus Christ] has borne our griefs and carried our sorrows; yet we esteemed Him as stricken, smitten by God and afflicted". This means that when Jesus was crucified, beaten and stricken for our sins, He was also taking on the pain and sorrows that we would have to deal with in the future. God is all-powerful. He has the power to take away your pain and heal your heart, making you a new creation. God makes ALL things new and nothing is impossible for Him. If you are hurting today because of the sins of someone else, God is calling out to you and telling you that He is the only answer to your pain, to your sorrow and to your wounds. His desire is to have a relationship with you and to be a true father figure; a father figure who will never hurt you, who will never abandon you, and who will fill you with a love that cannot compare to any other love found in this world.

On the other hand, this poem also addresses the issue of judgment being passed on people. What was your first impression of the speaker of the poem when you read "age eighteen"? Be honest. You probably thought she was conceited and self-absorbed. But the bible says in Matthew 7:1 "Do not judge, or you too will be judged". Sometimes we come across people who we really just want to stay away from because they come off as conceited, or rude, etc. But the fact of the matter is that we really don't know what people have gone through or experienced in their lives. We cannot under any circumstances pass judgments on people. It is simply not our job to do so. The only judge is God and His commandment is for us to love others as ourselves. When we make mistakes it is very easy to come up with excuses to justify our actions. Why then, is it so hard for us not to pass judgments on others? Instead of judging, we should be taking the time to share God's love with people who are having difficulties in life. When in doubt about how to react ask yourself the most simple question; what would Jesus do? How would He treat this person?

I also want to address the issue of child abuse. In Matthew 18 Jesus introduces the idea that believers must be as little children in order to enter into the kingdom of heaven. He refers to the believers as "little ones", but I also believe He is literally making a statement about the children. In Matthew 18:6 Jesus says, "If anyone causes one of these little ones to stumble, it would be better for them to have a large millstone hung around their neck and to be drowned in the depths of the sea". He goes on to say in verse 10, "See that you do not despise one of these little ones. For I tell you that their angels in heaven always see the face of my Father in heaven". I genuinely believe that God has a special connection to children because they are innocent. When Jesus makes these statements about anyone bringing harm to a child, they are almost said as a warning. The bible teaches us that vengeance belongs to God and that He is the one who avenges us (Romans 12:19). If God is willing to avenge us and we are sinners, how much more will He avenge a child who is innocent and has no sin.

This brings me to my last point. A situation like this can make the victim want to seek revenge and fill themselves with hatred for the person who abused them. However, the bible tells us not to take revenge but to leave room for God's wrath because He is the one who repays (Romans 12:19). The bible also says that we must forgive in order to be forgiven. Mark 11:25 states "And whenever you stand praying, forgive, if you have anything against anyone, so that your Father also who is in heaven may forgive you your trespasses." In a situation of sexual abuse, forgiving is probably the hardest thing to do. It may take time but be aware that if you want God to forgive your trespasses, you too must forgive the person who harmed you. But do not fret, God will give you the strength you need to do so. You must ask God to increase His love in you. Only with His love will you be able to forgive the person who harmed you. Once you are able to forgive, God can lift the burden of hurt that you have inside and you can move on to fulfill the beautiful purpose that God has for you. It doesn't have to be easy, but know that with God ALL things are possible (Philippians 4:13).

Words of the Silent

I turn my music up loud, wondering, maybe if I turn it up enough someone might notice I'm crying out. I'm drowning in my thoughts but my words live in a drought. My actions give me away but I inspire no doubts in those who walk by me as if I were imaginary. I feel so isolated at times, even with my family and its absurd. Their own voices they'd prefer a million times before I'm heard. It's not that they don't care. I guess their vision has been blurred so that I am now invisible and only I can hear my words. Only I feel this hurt. I said I'm over the rejection, the neglect, and imperfections!

Did anyone hear me?! Seems I'm shouting at my own reflection. Great deception, what I feel, knowing no one seems to pay attention. We all live in the same house but somehow in different dimensions. Because I see them, they see me, but there's no acknowledgment of this tension. I'm alone in the end, just wish someone would pay attention. So I cut deep into my skin, wishing, hoping, wondering, if maybe I'll feel something. Anything. Even the slightest sting. Will there even be blood when inside I feel so empty?

Will anyone notice the scars I bear on my arms? Will anyone notice I'm doing myself harm? Do I need to ring an alarm, and wear a sign on my head that reads "I feel dead"? Or should I keep my silence instead and keep dangling my life on this thread hoping for the pain to end? One thing's for sure, one day my words WILL be heard. Because I'll keep reaching out to those who dare to come near me, to those who won't fear me, and to those who are willing to guide me and rear me. My lips are silent now but my actions speak clearly, because my silent words I'll be screaming until the whole world hears me...

Reflection: "Words of the Silent"

This poem is targeted at youth. Many teens and young adults are cutters. I'm saying this as bluntly as I can. It's a very common issue and it's time to address it. Maybe there's an inner pain that you're trying to get out but deep down inside you know, the pain isn't really going anywhere no matter how deep you cut. But guess what? Jesus Christ already carried with that pain. Every cut you've inflicted on yourself, He already had to deal with when He was stricken before dying on the cross. Isaiah 53:5 says that "the punishment that brought us peace was upon Him, and by His wounds we are healed". The wounds Christ suffered and the punishment He had to take, gave us peace and healing in return.

His love for you is immense and even if you feel like you're alone and no one cares, the bible says that God will **never** leave you nor forsake you (Deuteronomy 31:6). NEVER. You are not alone. That is a lie directly from the enemy. Before Jesus was taken back to heaven, He said to His disciples "And surely I am with you always, to the very end of the age." That promise was not only to His disciples, but also to all those who believe in Him. Jesus is with you always and He will not leave you in your time of need. Even when you feel like He is far away He is there for you.

So you don't have to feel alone, you don't have to feel like no one understands your pain. God fully understands and comprehends you. He knows you better than you know yourself. Ephesians 1:5 says that God predestined us to be His adopted sons and daughters because it gave Him pleasure. To be predestined means that before the beginning of the world God had already thought of you in His mind and He loved the idea of you so much that He created you. So I don't care if anyone told you that you're worthless or that you don't matter. God created you with a purpose and He loves you. In fact, you mattered to Him so much that He was willing to send His son to die on the cross for you. You are not forgotten. The Creator of the whole universe is your Father and He loves you more than you can imagine. So maybe it's time you stop drawing blood, and instead accept the blood that was already shed for you on the cross. Accept God's healing, accept His salvation and accept His love. He has bigger and better plans for your life. So don't let your circumstances or the people around you define you. Let God, your Creator, define you.

Sinner

Sinner…

That's what they call me. But I don't recognize the name.

They say I sold my body for a little bit of fame.

But they must be wrong, for the girl inside me doesn't recognize the reflection of the woman I became. On my forehead I see a mark clearly stained; it says, "BLAME". Others seem to see it and don't care, but maybe if they knew my pain, maybe if they knew my story, they wouldn't condemn me to flames. All the same, they say I'm no dame, but instead I'm a…

sighs

Dare I say the word that burdens me in shame?

"You're a prostitute!" they exclaim. Then they assault me with degrading names. I can't seem to escape.

Until one day those names I accepted and that label I became, losing my identity and the name they defamed.

Now I'm sure I've hit rock bottom. There's a price for my death and my head is wanted on a silver plate.

But then I hear a voice call out to me and say, "Greater is the name…"

And all of a sudden my body is in a trembling state, my hands begin to shake, my voice cracks and I stutter to say "w-what?"

The voice replies, "I said greater is the name. Greater is the name of He who the price has paid, whose blood was shed for your life to be saved. He wipes away your blame, lifts the burden of your shame, purifies your name, calls you His daughter and takes away

your pain. So to those who condemn you, this is what you'll say...
"Greater is the name of Jesus who saves, than the sin that *once* kept me enslaved, but today inside His book of life He has written MY name...

Reflection: "Sinner"

This poem is a modern retelling of the bible story of the woman caught in adultery that Jesus rescued from being stoned in John 8. It is said that the woman was a prostitute. So, there's a few things I want to address with this poem. This poem carries the theme of a "name". It begins with the woman being called a sinner. She is then called a prostitute and later other degrading names.

I want to address the issue of degradation of women through name calling. In the media and in music it is all too common for women to be called an array of degrading names. It's come to the point where women call each other these names as a joke or as a term of endearment. Women this should not be. Do not accept such terms when being spoken to. We need to overcome these degrading names. Women have worked so hard in America to be able to obtain an education, to be able to vote, to be able to own property in their own name, etc. We have come a long way and we cannot allow ourselves to be degraded or to be treated as lesser beings by our modern society.

Now, to women who do engage in prostitution, I do not condemn you just as Jesus did not condemn this woman in the bible. I realize that sometimes the circumstances that lead women to prostitution are extremely difficult ones. What I tell you is this: You were not made to be a prostitute. You were made to be a daughter of God, a woman of dignity, a beautiful woman. God still has a plan for your life. If you entered into the world of prostitution due to financial necessity, know that one of God's many names is Jehovah Jireh which means God will provide. God can and will provide you with the way out of that world. Trust in God. Give Him your heart, let Him rescue you from that world and let Him heal you.

You are not forever meant to be in the position that you are currently in. You do not have to live with the label of prostitute. This is what the Lord says to you today, "Do not fear for I have redeemed you; I have summoned you by name; You are mine" (Isaiah 43:1). You belong to God! Your body doesn't belong to anyone else. It's time to reclaim your body, to reclaim yourself. To become the woman you were predestined to be. It's not over yet. Let God work a miracle in your life. Accept Him, ask Him for forgiveness and ask Him for His divine intervention in your life. You are not alone. Reach out to someone. Even I am willing to listen and seek help for you. My contact information is at the end of this book. But don't give up. God is trying to rescue you today. Let Him!

Be Still

It's a thick pain coming from within my chest. My heart is crying out wanting this torment to end. My womanhood I defend as I feel the lump in my breast. My fingertips I press against the reason for my stress. And depressed is not the word. To lament is what I yearn and as my days become more blurred it seems my prayers go unheard.

This disease is so absurd. From life itself I am deterred. Only shame covers my hurt when others pity this flightless bird. To my reflection I am humbled. Where once stood a strong woman, I see walls that crumble. I mumble when I speak and tumble when I walk the streets. I'm not that woman of high self-esteem that in the photographs laughs at me. The fiery passion of what could've been has all but died and left debris. Unbreakable to the human eye I seemed, but the soul within me cries out "Please take this curse from me!" But silence replies and inside I freeze. Cold becomes my heart. In bitterness I fall apart, but something lingers in my heart...

Yes, something lingers and its strong. Something I abandoned for so long. It's disguised as a hopeful song pouring from my lips. I can't hold on. I can't contain the tears. This joy I must prolong. Faith is what captures me inside, what I was missing all along. Yet they claim that I am wrong, that miracles do not exist. But I know now to be strong and with my faith I will persist. For the doctors do not know the God who heard the prayers from my lips. And with all my strength I will resist and let the world remember this: that I will be still and know that He is God, my Redeemer, my Healer, and HE STILL LIVES!

Heart Beat

I heard his heart beat once.
But that was long ago.
Back when I didn't know the miseries that life would hold.
Before the dreams and mysteries of life grew cold.
Just like the hole that I carry in my soul.

Emptiness…
Is what takes hold when decisions are made with consequences unknown. Then the bitterness grows and life unfolds. It isn't pretty like I was told. Young age plus bad decisions only brought responsibilities I wasn't ready to hold. The expectation to fit the mold of a mother responsible for another soul; it was a burden far beyond my control. But reality struck when that belly began to grow. I wasn't old enough, wise enough or mature enough to know. But my womb cried out to me begging me, "No, mom don't do it!"

I wonder what if and what could've been, if I didn't submit to the pressures of all the arguing. Mom and dad think I screwed up. My boyfriend refuses to step up. What would've happened if I didn't give up? But all the what if's don't really mean much, if what once grew inside me is now buried in dust. And I feel his infant breaths with every wind gust, his tears with every raindrop that my lips ever touched. I could've sworn I heard him say my name from inside my womb, begging and crying in distrust. He knows I heard him, that I told him to hush and that in my confusion I took his life and killed his trust.

And I know that he knows that I did…

I did hear his heart beat once.

Reflection: "Heart Beat"

This poem is in no way meant to judge any female who has ever had an abortion. In fact I wrote the poem in first person for that reason. I am in no way talking down to you if you've had an abortion. I know that having an abortion isn't an easy decision and that it can cause a heavy burden of guilt afterwards. I'm not going to sugarcoat this; an abortion is not pleasing in the eyes of God. However, after it is done, it's done and there's nothing you can do about it at that point. But God doesn't want you to live with the burden of that guilt forever. Part of the burden of our sin is guilt. When we commit a crime against God, we are burdened with the guilt of it. The purpose of guilt is to let us know when we've done something wrong.

Nevertheless, when Jesus died on the cross and carried the burden of your sin, He also carried the burden of guilt that came with it. If you truly repent of your sins, then God is gracious and merciful to forgive you and take the burden of your guilt. Once God forgives us, we no longer have to feel guilty. If God is holy, perfect, almighty and powerful and He is able to forgive us, then we should also forgive ourselves.

This following part does not apply to all women who have had abortions, as there are many reasons women obtain abortions. However, if the unwanted pregnancy that resulted in abortion occurred because the female was sexually active without being married then we must find a way to stop this from happening again in the future. The answer is purity or celibacy. I realize that the world has convinced us that sex outside of marriage is the norm. But God holds us to higher standards. Corinthians 6:19-20 states, "Do you not know that your bodies are temples of the Holy Spirit, who is in you, whom you have received from God? You are not your own; you were bought at a price. Therefore honor God with your bodies." The bible teaches us that our bodies were bought by

Jesus Christ when He died on the cross.

Furthermore, God calls us His in the bible (Isaiah 43:1). We belong to Him and we are to honor Him with our bodies. You are special to God, and He wants you to only give your body to the man whom He has chosen as your perfect mate. God wants us to remain pure for our own benefit, so that things such as unwanted pregnancies don't occur. He wants us to live happy fulfilled lives but He wants us to live them in the right order. You are His daughter and as any loving Father, He wants the best for His daughters. Let Him in, let Him remove your burdens and guilt and let Him teach you what true love is.

Forgiven

You spoke to me today, and I didn't need to hear Your voice to know what You were saying. You sent me a message in the most intimate and loving way. You reminded me of something that I understood better in my childhood days; that You forgive me no matter how many times I've gone astray. You've erased my pain and shame. Where they once stood engraved, now lies an empty page. You've wiped my slate clean. I cry tears of joy and not of pain. For I'd heard that You could save but today I saw Your grace. Today You touched my heart with a one-word phrase...FORGIVEN.

Forgiven. It's amazing how that one word means so much when it's coming from You. All of a sudden something in the air shifted; a burden was lifted. I stand up right with the air of a princess. Where I was once a body that merely existed, today You blew life into this dust and now I am living. Living because You made a sacrifice that no one else would have given. Living because after three days in the grave, in all glory You were risen. "Father forgive them" were the words You spoke as you were stricken. A price you paid so that my name in your book would be written. Lord, I'm more than in love, I'm smitten. You're more than enough, more than sufficient. Who needs the world when You're the golden ticket?

Because of You I've moved forward. The past is now behind me. No longer is it an obstacle in my way, but a memory to remind me of where it was my Savior found me. You looked at me oh so kindly, radiant and smiling saying: "Behold I make all things new, for it is not yours but My timing. Not the dimness of your past, but My light that's shining. I have called you out of the world. But will you take My hand and walk beside Me? Will you stand for Me even if the world denies Me? Will you walk beside Me, even if the circumstances seem to defy Me? Will you have faith that I will do what I say? Because I'm your guaranteed protection, I'm your safe place. Those who condemned you walked away. I am your truth, I am your light, you're daddy, your King, who restores your life. I do not condemn you, you are forgiven in My eyes. You're daddy's little girl, of course I paid the price. Because that's what daddy's do, for a child they sacrifice. And you my precious daughter, you were worth the price".

Mirror, Mirror on the Wall

They say mirrors don't lie but do they tell the whole truth? Can they see the inside? Do they reflect the real you?

A princess once asked,
"Mirror mirror on the wall, who's the fairest of them all?"

The mirror replies,
"Well you *would* be if you weren't so tall, or maybe so small. If you weren't so skinny, maybe if you were thinner? You're getting a little thick around the middle. Maybe if you lost the hips and had plumper lips. If you straightened your hair, put a little make up here, a little there. I see some wrinkles around your eyes. Let's not get started on those thighs. Maybe it's the way you dress; you should show a little more flesh. Wear some make up, get more sleep, exercise more, watch what you eat. Wear some contacts, your eyes are so plain! Get a tan, you could use a few shades. If you just forget everything and focus on that face, I'm sure the next time you ask I'll give you your place. You'll be the fairest of them all, a real princess with grace".

The princess glared at her reflection, and squinted her eyes, "but mirror" she said, "didn't you look at the inside? My Father the King, says that's the real prize, that's where the real beauty lies. Not on the outside where people wear their disguise, where they cover up the truth with lies, and wear layers of makeup to hide what's on the inside. Mirror, Daddy says I should be proud of the body He assigned, that I am perfect the way He made me, and there was no flaw in His design. It is Him who decides, the color of my hair, skin, and eyes, and He loves me more and more for who I am on the inside, not the outside. For He made me to reflect Him in all, it doesn't matter if I'm short or tall. So if your intention was to see me fall, it looks like I'm still standing for the long haul. You seem to have been deceived. Maybe you should give Daddy a call because quite frankly mirror, at your response I'm appalled. So I have one last question for you if you can answer and not stall… Mirror, Mirror on the wall, do you tell the truth at all?"

Reflection: "Mirror, Mirror on the Wall"

This poem talks about the issue of self-image; how we see ourselves. The mirror represents society. Society sends us many mixed messages about how we should look. Trends are constantly changing and many times the rapid changes leave women feeling inadequate and confused about how they look. It is one thing to want to be physically healthy and another to want to look as thin as the models in magazines. The fact is society holds us to expectations of beauty that simply are not realistic. The majority of women in America do not look like the models on TV or magazines. We as a culture have set and accepted standards of what women should look like that are unrealistic. They are standards that we cannot reach. If we are to change what we see, then we must change what we believe.

The bible teaches us that we are daughters of God (1 John 3:1-3). We also know that the work of God's hands is wonderful. We are fearfully and wonderfully made (Psalm 139:14). Genesis 1:27 says that men and women were created in the image and likeness of God. We also know that God is perfect (Matthew 5:48). The conclusion is that if we were created by God to look like Him and He is perfect and the work of His hands is wonderful, then He created us exactly the way He intended us to look and it was no mistake. My pastor always says that he imagines that when God created Adam in the garden of Eden He looked at Himself in the mirror as He molded mankind. How beautiful it is to think that God wanted so badly for us to be His sons and daughters that He said to Himself, "I want them to look like me too!" We should be satisfied with the work of His hands. I am not saying we should not wear makeup or do our hair, etc. What I am saying is that even without the hair and the makeup we should be satisfied with ourselves and happy with the way we look. We are beautiful in God's eyes inside and out. He created us and He loves us just the way we are. So who are we not to love ourselves? You ARE beautiful! Start believing it!

What it Means to Be a Dad

Any guy can be a father, but it takes a man to be a dad.
Being a dad means…
Coming home to children screaming "Daddy!" when your face
peaks through the door

Being a dad means…

Always remembering your kids as little boys or little girls

Being a dad means…

Watching what God has placed in your hands develop and unfold.

Being a dad means, a responsibility that never gets old.

But here we go, daddy, being my dad means that you made the
decision to be a part of my life

Being my dad means loving me even on the days when I put up a
fight.

Being my dad means running to CVS with me because it's that
time of the month.

Being my dad means giving me that hug I needed to keep moving
on.

Being my dad means getting a text early in the morning saying
daddy pray for me I'm about to take my finals.

Being my dad means showing up to my graduations to watch me
walk down the aisle.

Being my dad means always saying the right things to make me
laugh and smile.

Being my dad means, editing my poems even when you already have so much on your plate.

Being my dad means believing in me and teaching me to have faith.

Being my dad means being my example of God's love and His embrace.

Being my dad means you're the one man on this earth I can never replace.

Reflection: "What it Means to Be a Dad"

This is a poem I wrote to my dad a couple of father's days ago. It is a wonderful thing to have a good relationship with your earthly father, but I realize that this is no longer a common thing in today's world. I myself didn't always have a great relationship with my dad. There are many children that live without their dads. With divorce rates so high in the United States, it is easy to comprehend that many children live in households where only one parent is present. This just proves how strongly the enemy is attacking the family unit. So what's my point? Fathers, whether you live with your kids or not you NEED to have a relationship with your kids. You NEED to be an active part of your children's lives. You have no idea what a difference this makes.

On the other hand, ladies, the fact of the matter is that if your dad wasn't a part of your life it makes it harder to have a relationship with God. Why? Because part of the Trinity of God is a Father figure. Jesus taught us to pray, "Our Father who is in heaven". God is your father. Psalm 127:10 states "Though my mother and father forsake me, the Lord will receive me". God wants to be the Father figure in your life and He wants you to trust Him. He wants to have a father-daughter type of relationship with you. I realize that it is difficult to trust when your earthly father has let you down but God doesn't want you to think of Him the way you think of your earthly Father.

God will not forsake you, He will not abandon you, He will not ignore you, He will not forget you. God says in the bible, "Can a mother forget the child at her breast and have no compassion on the child she has borne? Though she may forget, I will not forget you!" –Isaiah 49:15. What I love so much about this verse is that even in His example, God acknowledges the fact that He cannot really be compared to a human parent's love because even they fail, but He will not fail. How amazing is that reaffirmation from God. He wants you to have that father-daughter relationship with Him. He wants to hold you and embrace you when you're crying and feel alone. He wants you to know He's always been there for you. Whether you felt Him or not He was and still is there. Right there where you are right now, God is with you, and you are His daughter. If you couldn't have a good relationship with your earthly Father, God is offering you the chance to have the best father-daughter relationship with Him. His arms are open for you. Will you climb into them?

-4-

Passing Faces

The poems in this section are about everyday people; the kind of people you may pass on the street, or people you may walk by but never really notice. These are their stories. Some of these stories are based on real people and/or real observations and others are fictional. Yet, the point I'm trying to make with this chapter is that those strangers you walk by on the streets are not just passing faces. They are souls; potential brothers and sisters in Christ. I find that especially in the north eastern part of America, people are very independent, to the extent that they don't notice things going on around them. Too many of us walk around with headphones plugged into our ears and sometimes miss the opportunity to speak to someone who is in desperate need of Jesus.

But we have to live life intentionally. The great command that Jesus gave us before leaving this world and ascending back to heaven was to go and preach the gospel all over the world. Part of our purpose is to spread the Word of God and we should be doing that on purpose by seizing every opportunity we get to speak to others. We just don't know when we may be the only ray of light in someone's life. I'm not saying we need to preach to everyone we see. But it is our job to notice and to be an example of love in people's lives.

In Matthew 22:39 Jesus confirms that the second commandment after loving God above all things is to love your neighbor as yourself. According to the oxford dictionary, a neighbor is "a person or place in relation to others, near or next to it". That means that anyone who gets near you is the neighbor that Jesus said you need to love as much as yourself. So let's stop looking at people as just passing faces and let's realize that we are all the same under God and are all in need of God's love and grace in our lives. Let's be intentional in our day to day living.

The Man with the Harmonica

His Harmonica he played. Sweet melody, music reached out to me like sun rays penetrating my skin on a summer day. I observed from a distance not too far away, an old man with gray hairs running down the sides of his face. An old coat he wore, worn by the time of his days. Aged, was the expression on his face. Engraved by the memories of his pain were moments of rage, disdain, and a path not paved. But with pride his harmonica he played.

On the corner of Main street on a chilly day, in front of him a small box he laid with the expectation that for his music someone might pay. Perhaps a dollar, a quarter, any kind of change. Anything to quench his deep hunger if only for a day. And people walked by with the self comfort that he would be okay, that someone else would pay, or that he'd only use the money for some drugs later that day. But those negative perceptions did not make him go astray. His pride still remained as I stood feet away, and his harmonica he played...

So I looked again. Then looked away when in my pocket I felt some change and a dollar I had saved. But I thought to myself, "give this away? But what about bus money for the next day? And do I care what people say? If I give him the dollar won't they judge me anyway? But it WOULD be a good deed to demonstrate. But maybe if I look away I won't have to see his melancholic face. The bus should be coming soon anyway."

But the harmonica no longer played. So I looked his way only to see an empty space where his box once laid. I looked around until I saw his face and there he was crossing the street towards his next destination of the day. And inside I felt ashamed. To my dismay he walked away to a better place. A place where people pay with no debate, and its innate to help those in need of hope and faith. But I stood in place, now farther away from the man with the harmonica that so beautifully played, that song that no one knew except the soul behind that darkened face.

And so I too went on my way, feeling the burden of my shame. And his harmonica became the purpose of what I write today. And even though the next day I lost the dollar I should've gave, I know that man still has his pride when his harmonica he plays.

That Bottle

He drops his bottle as he trips over a brick on the streets of downtown, rich with the stench of a minority beat down, whipped by the ignorance that his mind does crowd. Down bend his knees toward the dirt of the ground. Down goes his dignity because he was once proud. So he picks up that bottle that he filled with his doubts. THAT BOTTLE in which his security is found. THAT BOTTLE in which his worries he drowns. THAT BOTTLE, the excuse for his pain and his doubt. THAT BOTTLE, the companion that's never let him down. THAT BOTTLE that's become a living verb and not a noun, because it's a way of living in this ghost of a town filled with people giving the ugliest of frowns.

But though he hides the bottle well in his coat tucked inside, his breathe reeks and smells of the stench of demise. Not much of a disguise for the pain that he hides. Rejected, ignored and pushed to the side, redness lives around the pupils of his eyes. He's diminished the clarity and meaning of life. His clothes are proof of his long restless nights, smelling of must and covered in grime. His words he slurs when in strangers he confides, telling them the miseries of his dreadful life.

But no one listens to this guy. They just keep walking on by. And his addiction he denies, although his bottle is his pride. He slips through the cracks of life and his skeletons come to life. So he drinks them away one at a time. But time's not on his side and slowly he poisons his insides until his last tears he cries and woefully dies. And no one seems to pay mind. His death certificate goes unsigned, because his name no one could find. And all he ever left behind was that bottle of demise.

The Other Side of the Wall

They say the walls have ears. Isn't that the truth, because I can hear her tears from the other side of this room. From the other side of this wall I can hear it all. See I know how her loneliness her soul consumes, how she must feel so ugly on the inside but has to wear a costume. Because every night he walks into that room, he eats her food; he uses her and then leaves the same way he came in through.

It's a clear routine but I don't question why she doesn't leave. It's clear that she depends on this man, at least financially.

And I hear her leave for work every day but I imagine she doesn't make enough for her bills to get paid. In fact, I hear her argue with this man over money every day. Over that or the fact that for the night he never stays. She tells him she loves him as she begs for him to remain. I curse these walls for letting me witness so much pain! Yet, I listen with intent every single day, wondering if I'll ever knock on her door and say, "You don't need this guy, just walk away!" But then the doubts set in and I'm frozen in my cowardly ways. Or maybe I'm just afraid that she'll reject my help and stay the same.

But then I hear her pray as she cries to God desperately saying:

"I can't do this anymore! Why do I need to depend on him? Why can't I support myself? Why oh God do You delay? Can't You at least make him stay so this emptiness will go away? I hate this situation! He walks into my home, takes what he wants like a buffet and leaves as my trust he betrays over and over every day. I feel like a prostitute living this way! But I depend on his money. He's the reason I can pay for the roof over my head, for the food in my fridge. Please just help me, I can't keep living this way!"

And that was it. She was asking for help and I heard it. I'd been wasting my time thinking I was unfit to help this woman, but this tug in my heart I can't omit, I can't ignore it. I know it's God who's tugging on it. I must admit it's me He's chosen.

I still hear her crying on the other side of the wall. She's asking God "will no one answer my call?" So I walk over, stand in front of her door and try to stall. But I knock, and I wait feeling so self-conscious and small. Yet, still I wait, wondering what I'm going to say. Maybe I shouldn't have come at all. But just as I'm about to walk away, I hear footsteps approaching towards the hall. She opens the door, wipes the tears from her face and asks "can I help you?" But I hesitate, so I pray inside my mind saying, "Lord You know it all". Then I open my mouth to speak and say, "I'm here to answer your call…"

NOTE: This poem can and has been performed as a skit.

View at: http://www.youtube.com/watch?v=rOC1gUHObOo

Empty Space on the Wall

That empty space on the wall; that space that makes all her fears crawl like spiders creeping from the closet tormenting her 'til nightfall. Memories, that's all. Memories that come when she looks at that wall, at that void she can't fill even by building up all her will. She sits by the window sill and stares hoping her tears will fill the emptiness so tall. It's so vast and it's so sad and it's so past. But she relives that night every time she goes past that empty space on the wall. And who can say anything? Who can stop the pain it brings every time that wall she sees? Inside her heart she feels a sting, and it's the memories it brings of a boy who was fifteen; a boy with dreams. His eyes did gleam when he would smile but screams are all his mom can seem to see between that smile.

Empty is that space that his diploma would have filled; a space that should've never been if her son had not been killed. And looking at that empty space, up her spine brings such a chill. For her son didn't die because of sicknesses or being ill. He didn't die of old age nor did he die of free will. But life was taken from his lips and his dreams went unfulfilled; dreams to go to college and become a doctor, to protect the helpless and the ill. But instead of a right hand to the heart to take a Hippocratic oath, he held his right hand to his chest covered in blood and bullet holes. And while he took his final breathe, his mother could've never known. For she was buying him a gift, his birthday would've been tomorrow. What torment she must feel dealing with all of her sorrow.

But that wall is still empty waiting for her son's diploma. A request that was denied by death's discrete aroma. She cried and begged for it to be a dream, just a nightmare that her mind had schemed because her son didn't deserve to be caught up in this scene. He didn't drink, he didn't smoke, he never lied, he didn't cheat. He didn't waste all of his time roaming in the city streets. He was just at the wrong place at the wrong time, caught in the middle of a bad thing, mistaken by his physique. And not a day passes in that home in which that mother doesn't see that empty space on the wall that haunts her in her sleep; that space that shatters all her memories and devours all her dreams. And every so often she cries out and screams, "Why did you take him away?! Why couldn't it be me?!"

Break the Silence!

4 out of 5 teens who attempted suicide have given clear warning.

How many do you think have died this morning?

With their mental suffocation, detrimental frustration, judgmental conscience pushing towards their isolation.

Frowns wear their faces. Scars that clearly leave traces. What use to be smiles and embraces, depression now replaces. No progression but disgraces of discontent humiliation. It's sad and yet we turn our faces.

Do we not hear the warning signs? Shall they cry tears but have no ears incline? Shall we wait until they choose to die to say, "I knew something was wrong with that guy"? Or shall we break the silence and speak our minds, reporting what we've seen to substitute for late sighs? Because we forget time is not a thing money can buy. When it's too late, who stands up to the plate and says, "I tried"? No one. For we all turn our eyes.

We're only seeing what we want to see. We ignore the songs of their depressing CD's and the fake smiles of their repressed identities, the giving away of their belongings and the depressing thoughts behind their diaries. They're no longer enthused by school activities, but that of course we do not see. And for that our lips are mute and do not speak.

But today it ends! For the teens of our descent are killing themselves in silent torment. No time to repent for all the things they resent. Their faces are covered with death; what their souls learned to reflect. See, no one worried about where they went on the nights when new ways to die they would invent. If only someone had spoken out without being hesitant, or if their personal time someone had spent. But that personal time was at zero percent. So before another dies because unknowingly we gave consent, lets speak up this time and BREAK THE SILENCE!

Reflection: "Break the Silence"

"Break the Silence" is a poem addressing the issue of teen suicide. I wrote this poem as a cautionary poem to people who could potentially be in contact with someone who is suicidal. Many times we don't even notice the signs. If we do notice the signs we're too scared to ask or we think it's none of our business.

There seems to be an epidemic of teen suicide in the world. The enemy has for too long lied to our youth about who they are. He has stripped them of their true identities and convinced them that they are worthless, alone, unloved, hopeless, insignificant, having no purpose or potential for greatness. But this is simply a lie of the Devil to convince youth to kill themselves along with the purpose that God has placed in them.

To those who have considered suicide:

The bible teaches us that our true identity is that of sons and daughters of God. (1 John 3:1-3). The enemy will have us carry a burden of rejection on our backs, but the fact of the matter is that Jesus Christ was rejected first. You don't have to feel like no one understands what it feels like to be rejected because Christ was rejected by His own people, those whom He came to save. Is it fair? No. But the enemy has managed to twist the world to do his wicked will. Nevertheless, the good news is that there is hope for your life. You are not hopeless. In Jeremiah 29:11 it says, "For I know the plans I have for you, declares the Lord, plans for welfare and not for evil, to give you a future and a hope". There is a hope for you.

You are not worthless. This is who the bible says you are in Christ:

- You are a chosen people, a royal priesthood, a holy nation, God's special possession (1 Peter 2:9).

- You are a saint, a holy one (Ephesians 1:1)

- You are a new creation (2 Corinthians 5:17)

- You are the Righteousness of God (2 Corinthians 5:21)

- You are the temple of the Holy Spirit (1 Corinthians 6:19)

- You have been bought with a price. You belong to God. (1 Corinthians 6:19-20)

- You have been redeemed and forgiven of all your sins (Colossians 1:14)

- You are Christ's friend (John 15:15)

- You can find grace and mercy to help you in your time of need. (Hebrews 4:16)

- You are a citizen of Heaven (Philippians 3:20)

- You are complete in Christ (Colossians 2:10)

- You have not been given a spirit of fear, but of power, of love and a sound mind. (2 Timothy 1:7)

- You cannot be separated from the love of God (Romans 8:35-39

- You are redeemed...You are His! (Isaiah 43:1)

I Am the Voice

I am the voice:

The voice of a grandmother worn by her age,

The voice of insecurity seeking its last days.

Because instead of age that should be golden, it is rage that I am holding.

It is pain that fills my eyes every time that I avoid you. It's my tears that fill the sky every time you leave the room.

How easily they deceive you

And smile when they receive you

With their make believe stories that never took place.

But the reality of my memories is nothing but disgrace.

They kick me, they punch me and spit in my face

when you turn around and leave me, not returning for days.

Sometimes they don't feed me when I "misbehave". I don't know how much more neglect and isolation I can take. They mistreat me because I cannot speak for myself but the soul inside me cries out for help.

I am weak, so they take advantage of me. And the precious gifts you bring me, they steal and they keep. Even my bible I cannot read. And it is always dark, for through the closed shades, no light creeps. Even the sun hides from me. In this room there is no joy, only the memories of a life once enjoyed. I look at my reflection. It is not my own. Wrinkles and depressions, my reflection shows. So for those who can listen to my voice, don't allow this to happen by choice.

Look once and you will see what they want you to see.

But look twice, carefully, you might be looking at me.

Reflection: "I Am the Voice"

This poem is an awareness poem about elder abuse. In our current society as people are reaching longer life spans, a new phenomenon has come about; the "sandwich generation". The sandwich generation is a term developed to explain the phenomenon of the generation of people who are raising children but are also responsible for caring for their aging parents. Life has become so busy and complex that many times parents are placed into nursing homes as they may require more care than their children are able to provide. While nursing homes can be a great place for the elderly where they can connect with people who are their age and going through similar life experiences, the fact of the matter is that in some nursing/retirement homes abuse is occurring and often people are not aware of it.

Nevertheless, the bible gives us some guidelines on how we should treat our elders. First off, Leviticus teaches us to "stand up in the presence of the aged, show respect for the elderly and revere your God"(Leviticus 19:32). This is a direct command from God. He finishes it by saying "I am the Lord". In older times whenever a king would decree something he would stamp the decree with a symbol that represented him; kind of like a signature. I feel like that is what God is doing in this case. He is stamping this command with His signature at the end when He says "I am the Lord". Thus, as our King, God demands respect for the elderly.

The bible goes on to guide us in how we should treat the elderly in 1 Timothy 5:1 where it states, "Do not rebuke an older man but encourage him as you would a father." The bible tells us not to rebuke an older man. To rebuke means to express sharp, stern disapproval of, or to reprimand or scold. In other words it means not to speak harshly to an older person but to treat them with the same love, respect, compassion and encouragement that you would treat your own father with. If this is referring only to a simple rebuke, imagine how much more God disapproves of physical abuse to the elderly. The point being, abuse is NEVER okay. God expects us to treat the elderly with love and respect no matter what the circumstances. So I urge you, if you have an elderly family member or relative in a nursing/retirement home, be there for them, and take care of them. This is what pleases God.

Waiting to Exhale

I inhale. Smoke fills my lungs

leaving behind a bitter sweet taste on my tongue.

Bitter poison but sweet relaxation. I absorb into my bloodstream my own condemnation. I try to fight it but too strong is the temptation.

So strong the obligation to inhale once more and feed my starvation,

feed this addiction and play accomplice in my own assassination.

For I know that the pleasure I gain is not worth the contamination and pain.

But I continue in this flirtation with death,

inhaling once more and again.

Gambling on the day in which I'll hear the words say that my life is coming to an end.

But what will I do then? Who am I to blame when cheating death becomes my game every time that I inhale?

Why can't I change? I pray but still I'm the same.

They say it won't happen overnight, so in faith I remain.

But until then I inhale.

Still hoping that one day, with this addiction I can cope.

And maybe instead of inhaling and filling my lungs with smoke

I will inhale and God will be the one to fill my soul,

locking this addiction away in a bottomless black hole

so that I can finally take control and...Exhale.

Reflection: "Waiting to Exhale"

This poem is about the struggle some go through with addiction to cigarettes. But I want to address addiction to drugs in general. I know drug addiction is one of the most difficult habits to break; mostly because even if you don't want to continue it, your body asks for it. Paul relates to this when he talks about his struggle with sin in Romans 7:21-25. He says:

> "Here is the law I find working in me. When I want to do good, evil is right there with me. Deep inside me I find joy in God's law. But I see another law working in the parts of my body. It fights against the law of my mind. It makes me a prisoner of the law of sin. That law controls the parts of my body. What a terrible failure I am! Who will save me from this sin that brings death to my body? I give thanks to God. He will do it through Jesus Christ our Lord."

The point is that drugs are a sin against your own body. They are a form of destroying yourself and destroying the temple of the Holy Spirit (1 Corinthians 6:19-20). The reason it is difficult to stop this particular sin is because we have a law of sin that is working in our body even though in our minds we want to do the right thing. Nevertheless, look at how Paul ends his statement. He asks, who will save me from this sin that brings death to my body? Now I want you to replace the word "sin" with "addiction".

"Who will save me from this [*addiction*] that brings death to my body? I give thanks to God. He will do it through Jesus Christ." You must believe that God can help you to overcome any addiction and any temptation to continue using the drug. 1 Corinthians 10:13 says that "No temptation has overtaken you that is not common to man. God is faithful, and He will not let you be tempted beyond your ability, but with the temptation He will also provide the way of escape, that you may be able to endure it". Let God help you in the process. Remember you are not alone. The bible teaches that we should present our bodies as living sacrifices (Romans 12:1). The best way to give up an addiction is to just stop and sacrifice your body by not feeding it what it wants. Is it difficult? Is it painful? Yes! But the bible also says in Hebrews 2:18 that Jesus himself suffered when He was tempted and because of that He is able to help those who are being tempted. In your moment of temptation call out to Jesus and He will help you. Romans 8:26 also says that the Holy Spirit helps us in our weakness and He intercedes for us. That means the Trinity of God is working in your favor. Therefore, God is your way of escape! His plan and purpose for you is perfect and an addiction will not be enough to stop His purpose. So start removing the things that hold you back and start moving forward!

The Absence of a Father

A poem based on true events...

Fathers, be active in your children's lives because your mistakes are not their problem. Be aware of those eyes and ears that your example always follow. Because if love you fail to show, your child's heart will grow up hollow, and if he chooses to speak up one day, I'm sure your words he'll make you swallow. And the later the "I love you's" come, the more he'll hate being your son, the more it takes to be called father.

And that's the way the story starts if from outside you do follow...

Every day he rides the bus with mom and this new "uncle". On the way he goes to school, not knowing that his teen mom struggles. But he takes up his own seat right up front, sits on his knees as out the window he does peek and every so often he does speak, shouting, "Mommy the car, the truck, the street!" He points again and then he screams, "Mommy the bike, the bird, the leaves!" Yes everything amazes him; the whole world it almost seems; the whole world **except** one thing.

This stranger who walks on the bus, and mom's not too happy to see. "Don't you see your son?" she says, then he kisses the boy on the cheek. He says, "Hey son" then looks at the mother, "I'll stop by to see him next week". And on he goes, a day like any other and in the back he finds a seat. The boy keeps looking out the window, points outside and once again screams, "Mommy look, the sky, the grass, Mommy look a giant tree!"

And on goes the routine and on goes the routine, and tomorrow when the stranger comes, "Don't touch me!" is what the boy will scream.

Stranger with My Last Name

Who is this stranger who bears my last name, who wears a similar face but in my memories leaves no trace? In my heart he has no place, for I never felt the warmth of his embrace. Neither have I felt the need to desperately chase and find this man that from my mind, time has erased.

But I wonder...

Does he ever think about the son he misplaced? Or have I been forgotten just as I've forgotten him? Because all that I remember is mom working eight-hour shifts, slaving over a kitchen, working hard for what should've been a family trip. She worked hard for the clothes I'm in and to fulfill my every whim. But in this world that stranger does not exist. You see, he wasn't there for my first barber shop trim and he wasn't around to teach me how to ride a bike or swim. He was simply absent; a part of my past that's grim. So why would I ever want to know anything about him?

He wasn't there to watch me grow or teach me how to be a man. To me he's just another stranger I might've bumped into in my lifespan. Compared to the ocean he's just another grain of sand. At that, if I could compare life to a mall he'd be the unwanted name brand. He doesn't mean much to me. To him I was just another mistake unplanned; someone he could easily toss in the trash can, moving on with his life without looking back for one last glance. So why should I give him a chance? Why should I try to understand?

There's nothing more to be said, it's just a little too late. Forgive him? Maybe someday, but I'll always know he didn't contribute to the man that I became. I'll always remember that of me he was ashamed, that from me he walked away and that will never change. But God stepped in his place to make up for his mistakes, because any man can be a dad but a true father remains. So if you call yourself my father, I'm sorry that I have to say to me you're just a stranger...a stranger with my last name.

Reflection: "Absence of a Father" and "Stranger with my Last Name"

"Absence of a Father" and "Stranger with My Last Name" were both written from a male perspective. "Absence of a Father" is based on a true story. I actually did witness the situation occurring on a bus every day. It is about a younger boy. He was maybe 5 or 6 years old. "Stranger with My Last Name" is about what potentially happens later in life to that 5 year old boy.

Unfortunately, this is an all too common story. With divorce rates increasing, and the rate of teen pregnancy increasing, more and more children are being raised by single mothers and don't enjoy the benefits of a two-parent household. I urge fathers to be a part of your child's life. Even if you don't get along with the mother, establish your relationship with your son or daughter. Not only should you establish that relationship but you should be providing for them. The bible teaches in 1 Timothy 5:8 that "Anyone who does not provide for their relatives, and especially for their own household, has denied the faith and is worse than an unbeliever". God takes this matter extremely seriously. God is our spiritual Father and He provides for our every need (Philippians 4:19). Thus, fathers (and mothers) should make it an obligation to follow God's example in providing for their children.

To the child without a father, let God be the one who sustains you and teaches you how to be a man. I know that it is easy to be angry at your father for not being there when he should be, but holding all that anger in won't really do anything to him. It's only you who ends up hurting in the end. So I urge you to forgive. The bible teaches us "if you forgive other people when they sin against you, your heavenly Father will also forgive you"(Matthew 6:14). If you want to have a good relationship with your heavenly father that you weren't able to have with your earthly father, then you must learn to forgive. Then you will be able to allow God to fulfill that father role in your life and you'll be able to remove another obstacle on the road to fulfilling your purpose.

Common Courtesy: A Short Story

"Achoo! Achoo!! Achoo!!!"

Third time's the charm right? I hate sneezing in public. It's slightly embarrassing for me. My sneeze is very peculiar. I always sneeze at least three times; a series of small sneezes. Sometimes I can sneeze up to six times in a row. My grandpa use to tell me to just let it all out at once; as if one could control their sneeze. I don't think about how I'm going to sneeze when I do it. Do you?

Anyway, it just bothers me because sometimes people look at me funny. But mostly what bothers me is when no one even has the common courtesy to say, "bless you". I mean I just sneezed while standing at the bus stop in downtown. There were dozens of people around and not even one had the decency to say, "bless you". What happened to manners? Please and thank you's? Oh no, that's something of the past. It's like everyone is so wrapped up in their own lives and in their own thoughts that they can't walk out of their bubble for a few seconds just to say "bless you" to the person who just sneezed.

All I'm asking is that someone take off their headphones, unglue their eyes from their phones, and just notice that there are other human beings around living in the same world only a couple of feet away hoping for the slightest human interaction. And if that human interaction just so happens to be the kind words of a stranger saying "bless you" when someone sneezes, couldn't you just do it? Is that too much to ask?

"Achoo!" A little girl behind me stops in her tracks as she sneezes. She can't be more than seven or eight years old; probably on her way to school. "Achoo!" she sneezes a second time, once again being stopped in her tracks by her sneeze. I look at her as she continues to walk by. I turn around without saying anything.

Welcome to the world kid...

Reflection: Common Courtesy

I address two issues in this short story. The first issue I present is the one seen from the point of view is of the main character who is speaking. She contends with the matter of people being too preoccupied with their own lives to notice someone else. I think this is a sad reality. It truly is a problem. In the introduction of this chapter I spoke about loving your neighbor as yourself and about how anyone who gets near you is the neighbor that Jesus said you need to love as much as yourself. It is our responsibility to notice the people around us and be good neighbors. Our intentional actions towards another person could potentially be a ripple effect of change with no end to it. God goes out of His way to give us "God winks", as my good friend Leanna calls them. A "God wink" is another way of explaining God's grace through His intervention in our lives. Although we don't deserve it, He gives us that special attention. If God takes His time to notice us and give us His attention, why shouldn't we notice others and share that love of God with them in any way we can; even if it's as simple as saying "bless you" to someone?

The second issue I address with this short story is that if we want to see things change in the world, we cannot be contributors to the problem. The main character in this story goes on a rant about how bad it is that no one says bless you to her. Yet, when the opportunity presents itself for her to say bless you to someone else, she chooses not to do so. She becomes just as "bad" as the people she is complaining about. Mahatma Gandhi once said that "we must be the change we wish to see in the world". I completely agree with this statement. Sometimes we might think that something as small as saying "bless you" doesn't make a difference.

However, what if someone had said bless you to the main character in this story; would she have in turn said it to the little girl? Would the little girl have said it to someone else? I'm trying to address a bigger issue than just saying bless you; it's caring for others even if it's in the smallest way. I believe small deeds do make a difference. Even if it doesn't mean much to that person, our Father in Heaven sees our actions. The bible says in Ecclesiastes 12:14, "For God will bring EVERY deed into judgment, with every secret thing, whether good or evil." There is nothing we can do that God will not notice. Thus, we should not do these good deeds to gain recognition from man, but we should do them from the kindness of our hearts knowing that God sees all that we do.

We should be intentional in showing the love of God even if it's in a small deed. When we care about others intentionally, we are working on the purpose and commandment that God gave us of loving others as we love ourselves. So, be an example of God's love today! You never know how much of a difference it can make in someone's life.

-5-

The Controversial Chapter

I wrote this chapter on purpose with a purpose. Most of the poems are titled in a way that seems controversial and I did that intentionally to attract attention because the messages being sent are strong, powerful and very necessary. Some of the poems in this chapter are topics that are rarely addressed but need to be dealt with. If we don't talk about them, then they cannot be fixed. So before you begin this chapter, be advised that I am not sugarcoating anything in this chapter, but I firmly believe that it's time we talk about these things. So give this chapter a chance before you judge based on the titles. You might find yourself surprised.

The "F" Word

Why are so many Christians afraid of using the "F" word? As if it were a slur we avoid and prefer not to say it. So as not to offend anyone, we downplay it until our moral lines we blur. Do we just prefer to be seen and not heard? Or are we just afraid that people will think we're absurd? I mean what's so bad about using the F word? It's gotten to the point where we'd rather plead the fifth than let this word slip through our lips.

But let me explain myself a bit. The "F" word to which I refer is really simple; it's faith. And as Christians you would think we'd place it into practice every day. But as the fifth amendment of the United States claims, we choose to remain silent than for ourselves to incriminate. Are we afraid that the world against us will discriminate? Or do we discriminate against the world by not using our faith?

I guess we forget that it's them who need us; that their lives run the risk of eternal damnation and we're the ones who hold the keys within us. So why so much of the hush-hush? Shouldn't we be bold for Jesus in our schools? Shouldn't we be bold for Jesus in our lives? Shouldn't we proclaim our faith to the world instead of putting on a fake disguise? I mean who are we trying to fit in with; those who walk the path that's wide, or those who follow Jesus Christ? Don't you realize that faith is a servant that works in your favor at all times?

But you can't just believe it, you've got to declare it! You can't just say it, you have to act on it. Like a uniform you've got to wear it. Like it's food to a starving world, we must share it. Like it's a new born baby we must cherish it. Like it's the only comprehensible word in our language, we must communicate it.

Because the day is soon to come where we will each stand before

God the judge and give account for every word we spoke... and didn't speak. Every opportunity we were given and didn't take is a potential soul that didn't get saved. Do we not yet understand the urgency and purpose of our faith? Do we not yet see that it has the power to heal, save and liberate? On our tongues are the power of life and death, and our faith is life just waiting to be said. But don't forget, that even if we don't speak death, but choose to remain silent instead, and we assume everything will be alright, then it's the equivalent of holding the bloody knife. Because choosing to do nothing is still a choice. So if you want your master to rejoice, you've got to use your talents, you've got to use your voice.

So share your faith whenever the opportunity is open. Whenever you feel that tug in your heart telling you, "that's the person", speak to them without hesitation. Because even if they choose not to pay attention, you've planted a seed of faith somewhere in their heart's foundation. And if the seed you planted is the word of God, then there's no way it can return back to you void or flawed.

Just read Isaiah 55:11, not only does God Almighty decree it, but He clearly says it:

"So is my word that goes out from my mouth: It will not return to me empty, but will accomplish what I desire and achieve the purpose for which I sent it." –Isaiah 55:11

Indifference

Indifference blinds my generation with ignorance! It's a lack of concern, of attention and lack of interest for other people, for life, and for God in every sense. God calls out to them but they refuse to listen. They could care less about the troubles of the world and all that is wicked. It's all about self-love and giving into the flesh but what's the underlying reason? I've got to question this. It's not lack of motivation or lack of knowledge for what's out there. For you see, there is a difference, in order to be indifferent you must be aware and still not care. It seems that something's really wrong, something's just not right here.

Because we put ourselves first and fall slaves to self-love and greed. We start to say "forget the world it's all about me!" You say, "I'm doing me now" as your flesh you feed, but falling short of God's glory, your testimony becomes weak. Until you reach your peak of sinfulness ways, your me-ness begins to move up the chain. But meaningless is the rise to self-fame when your concern for the world goes up in flames. For you were not made to toot your own horn or be a cheerleader at your own game, but instead for His pleasure you were made. And He will not accommodate into the cramped space between the page of the bible that you only pick up for the service every Sunday. And then you wonder why it all goes wrong in this life that you're living. You're asking God to make a difference, when it's you who doesn't want commitment. You want Him to bless you and give you forgiveness, yet you refuse to walk away from wickedness. You run around thinking you're invincible and limitless, while death knocks at your door with a paycheck for your sinfulness.

Because we get ignorant when we train our eyes to see only what we want to see and we focus our vision on everything we want to be. We start to see only what's good, failing to notice iniquity, failing to speak up when we see or hear something wrong. And we even get indifferent listening to these songs. I guess it's ok for Jay-Z to say, "Jesus can't save" as long as there's a catchy beat to which we can sing along. And I wish I was wrong but this generation has let things slide for too long. Have we become mindless puppets that the media can string along? Or are we the body of Christ still standing strong?

Last time I checked God doesn't like lukewarm. So how is it we dabble a little here a little there, trying to get the best of both worlds? Yet, we are not of this world and its confirmed by the Word. But it seems our vision is blurred and we are no longer easily deterred from the ways of this earth. It seems we have conformed. Do we no longer fear God? Do our ears not hear God? Is he too old school for us now? Or is the ignorance blasting from our radios just too loud? Have we forgotten how to listen to God's whisper in our ears? Because His plan has been set before the creation of days, weeks, and years. But it seems that at this height what He needs are volunteers.

He seeks a generation willing to follow Him even if the world attacks us with sin-dipped spears, scares us with every kind of fear, tempts us with temporary laughter and cheer. For He seeks a strong people who will follow Him through anything and anywhere. But where are those people today? Their ears have filled with nonsense, their eyes are glued to television sets, their mouths have forgotten how to bless, their minds are filled with ignorance, and their hearts are lifted up in arrogance. But who will rise up and put a stop to this when our biggest problem is… indifference?

P.O.R.N

P: Pornography, poisoning people's minds, preventing predetermined purposes. Packaging predisposed sin, preparing people for worthlessness. Placing importance on practices that can only lead to hopelessness. Pretended perspectives of could-be perfection, posing the question what's holiness? Past progression to the point of oppression. Pure minds pushed past the point of obsession. We're overstepping in the Lord's private possessions. Suppression of purity, approaching transgression. While your point of view and perspective are pushing out toward depression. Perplexed you're beginning to question, are we pivoting right for dissension?

O: Or are we occupying our souls on obsessions? Opening doors only leading to obliteration. Obtaining orders for condemnation; self-praising and adoration only leading to deterioration. Overtly obstructing orders ordained by the owner of all creation. Overt and open objectification of women, overexposing our inner most limits. Only ostentatiously attempting to stay hidden. We're occulting from the Omega and His omnipotence. Over-justifying ourselves, over-supposing our limits, only omitting the fact that we're sinning because our flesh likes the pleasure we're getting.

R: But are we really remembering righteousness rendering His own life so that ourselves we're surrendering? I reiterate to respectfully remind you of the rights He has upon you. We retaliate by responsibly responding to His purity. Your body remains a reflection of Him; that's your security. But we resist; returning to our sin. Remaining in the end irresponsive and reluctantly relapsing, our will begins to bend. We reverse and backtrack the purpose we had, reemerging to our fallen state, forgetting that the Redeemer, blood had to shed.

N: Never neglecting the need to be perfected. Knowing what it is to be rejected. Not to mention, we're knowledgeable of right and wrong. We now need redemption, necessary attention from the one true God. Never forgetting we're never alone, never forgetting, never forgetting…

Our bodies are temples of the Holy Ghost.

Reflection: "P.O.R.N"

This may be one of the most awkward and confusing poems in the book. It addresses the topic of pornography through an acrostic poem that uses alliteration. Alliteration is when one uses the same letter or sound repeatedly. As you can see, each stanza begins with a letter that is used often throughout the stanza. I used alliteration as well because it requires repetition. An addiction tends to be a repetitive action that one does not desire to continue carrying out. So, the use of alliteration in this poem also functions as an underlying portrayal of the problem of being addicted to pornography.

I wanted to address the issue of pornography because it is a growing problem in the world. I chose to address it the way I did in the poem because it is, for many people, a "taboo" topic that's difficult to talk about. In order to understand this poem it requires a breakdown of the words and sentences. It's highly probable a reader might not understand it after giving it one read. Nevertheless, as ineffable as the subject is, it's time to speak up about it. The following statistics are from familysafemedia.com:

- From the year 2005 to the year 2006, pornography went from being a 12.62 billion dollar business to being a 13.33 billion dollar business in America.

- The pornography industry is larger than the revenues of the top technology companies combined: Microsoft, Google,

Amazon, eBay, Yahoo!, Apple, Netflix and EarthLink.

- The average age of first internet exposure to pornography is 11 years old.

- Worldwide on a monthly basis there are 72 million visitors to pornographic websites.

With these statistics it is pretty clear to see that pornography is a worldwide problem. Pornography is an addiction/obsession that completely contradicts the bible's plan and purpose for man-kind.

Sex is supposed to be a sacred thing reserved for marriage. The world has perverted this beautiful gift of God into a way of destroying the temple of the Holy Spirit. The bible teaches us that our bodies are temples of the Holy Spirit and that we are to glorify God with our bodies (1 Corinthians 6:19-20). Unfortunately, pornography is a problem that even affects Christians in the church today. I am not saying this to pass judgments but to raise awareness to the pornography viewer. Your relationship with God will be affected by this problem and in return you will be stunted in following the purpose God has for your life. Nevertheless, as with any sin or addiction, it can be broken and there is forgiveness (view reflection of "Waiting to Exhale" pg.65) and there is redemption in Jesus Christ. Let's be a pure generation for Christ.

Birds and the Bees

Ladies and Gentlemen,

Pay attention please. We need to have a little talk about the birds and the bees. It's a beautiful way to put it, to talk about with ease. But my intention here is not your comfort or for you to be pleased. So I'm going to be straight forward, no need to appease, and my first words go out to... all the young ladies:

Ladies Ladies, let's talk about respect. It seems this is something you're all too willing to forget. Whether it be that daddy is absent, physically or emotionally, it doesn't matter in the end. But that insecurity and neglect, is spotted a mile away by desperate men thinking of only one thing; to get between your legs. And if he does love you, he won't pressure you into sex. But a man with no respect will call you a tease if his offer you reject. And speaking of teasing, can we say we're completely innocent? Taking extra steps to show off your chest, pulling down that shirt to show the cleavage of your breasts, hiking up that skirt to expose a little more leg; going down this path, the wrong attention's what you'll get.

And you complain about love and how all men are jerks, but you don't stop to think about how the enemy works and how he uses sex to take away your self-worth. Then he deceives the world and tells them sex sells and so the media uses sexual images for your mind to overwhelm; to make you think that the physical is all men are interested in. That no man would ever pay attention to your spiritual wealth and that the only way they'll fall in love is if your naked with no strings attached. But in the end you're the one who's forsaken when your self-esteem they've snatched. So I ask you to hold on to your innocence and let yourself not be shaken. But stand with strength unmistaken and have the courage to say no until the day that by marriage you're taken.

On the other hand, gentlemen, it seems the definition of a man has been tampered with and you've been misled. Because your manhood is not measured by how many women you take into your bed but by how much wisdom and strength it takes you to follow the voice of God instead, when He tells you to wait until marriage. And the world may yell, "You don't know what you're missing out on!" But when you get a girl pregnant, it's you that same world frowns upon. The media tells you to look for big butts and breasts; that it doesn't matter what goes on inside her head as long as you get between her legs. So you get dumb inside your head, only paying attention during sex ed. Focusing too much on the size of her breasts, you don't want A's and B's, you prefer those C's and D's instead, and that of course is reflected in the grades that you get. And in turn your ignorance you project, and the voice of God you quickly learn to forget.

But people let's realize sex is not a bad thing. It's a creation of God meant for intimate bonding. It wasn't meant to be used as a one-night fling or in exchange for other things. Realize this dates back to Adam and Eve, to the day they became one flesh before the highest of Kings. It's a physical pact to bind for all eternity. Yet we use it in vain for a few minutes of ecstasy. Ladies and gentlemen, let's really think; saving it for your one and only, now wouldn't that be something? And for those who think it's too late because mistakes have already been made, just remember if one thing is true, our Father in Heaven makes ALL things new.

I Won't Compromise My Temple

This body I live in is not my own. It was bought with a price that I could never afford. A price that didn't need to be paid, that could've been ignored. And yet, in the Mighty One's inventory I've been accounted for. And therefore, I will not fornicate, masturbate, obliterate or disintegrate any part of this temple that is my body. I will not discomfort the Holy Spirit in His dwelling place regardless of what others may say or think about me. So I place into practice every day the words of first of Corinthians chapter six verse twenty, reminding me that I was bought with a price so I must honor God with this body.

Furthermore, I will not reduce my thinking to believe that love and sex are the same thing. Just like being text to say good morning isn't the same as being texted at two in the morning when he's not really thinking about me but he's just getting a little lonely. You see, I've witnessed all the warning signs; a million times I've heard this story. So I will not put on my makeup and lipstick in attempts to seduce a man who's thoughts are simplistic; only thinking of turning me into another "girl who got played after giving it away" statistic. Enough has happened, and enough is enough! I'm done sugar coating and fluffing it up! I've learned my lessons and I've come to know that my body is a temple on which I dare not foreclose. For I was chosen for God's purposes and not my own, and so…

I will not delve into the lustful unknown or throw myself into temptations that leave my heart feeling as empty as the deepest hole. I will not replace "glory to God's" and "hallelujahs" for meaningless groans and moans or for short-lived temptations that got me thinking I'm grown; only to end up in my bed alone filled with regrets and attempts at justifications when really all I want to do is look at my reflection and throw the first stone. But I remember that through his blood I've been atoned, that just because I've failed once doesn't mean I need to keep going down that road.

And so I will not give in! I will not let temptations win! I will not be that girl sitting in her room crying over some guy who didn't deserve my time and all the while watching my spirit dying. See I've learned that I'm worth much more than a one-night stand; that when Jesus died on the cross and outstretched His hands, He did it so that I could understand that while these other men have used me for their temporary pleasures and demands, He will never hurt me or abuse me because I'm in His eternal plans.

And so my vacant sign is off now because this temple has been sold and now has a new owner. He paid the ultimate price, not with gold but with His life, so that I could call Him my life donor. So I don't need to walk with my head towards the ground, looking like a loner. Because I've been chosen to represent my King, the Ultimate Restorer.

-6-

Let's Be Realistic

So the poems in this chapter are about the realities and struggles of being a Christian. It is not easy. It is a process. And it does take time. Becoming a Christian doesn't necessarily mean life gets easier in the blink of an eye. Christians still struggle. I know I still struggle, just like I'm sure you still struggle. But the purpose of this chapter is to let you know you're not alone. Some of the poems in this chapter are about me and my experiences and although it's never easy to open yourself up to strangers, I'm willing to do that. If as human beings we don't communicate with each other, if we don't empathize, if we don't take the time to hear someone else's story, we will never truly appreciate our own story and our own experiences. I pray that this chapter will enable you to open up with yourself and see where your relationship with God is and where other areas of your life could use some work. I know

I'm still a work in progress.

As a Christian you will struggle, you will have moments where it's hard to trust God; you will have moments where days pass in which you don't speak to God. It happens to the best of us. But it's no reason to give up. As long as you're still breathing there is always the opportunity to better your relationship with God and improve your life. Your purpose is waiting for you. God is waiting for you. He wants to do awesome and mighty things for you but the decision is ultimately yours. A relationship with God is not easy. You have to work at it like any other relationship. But I can guarantee you that life with Him is much sweeter than life without Him. It's not easy, but through Christ we can do all things (Philippians 4:13).

My Truth

I was born and raised in a Christian home. You'd think I lived my life in a sheltered dome away from the sin that the world has sown. And maybe I was sheltered, but at some point you grow prone to sin and when you feel alone that's when temptations and sin come along. It didn't take me too long to realize I too was made of flesh and bones. Yes, to me my sins are all too well known. I started doing things at an early age that were too grown. I learned to do what society taught and blamed it on my parents' divorce. But at some point I had to step up and take responsibility for my own.

See, there comes a time in every child's life where their parents' salvation no longer covers the bloody knife. At some point I realized I caused my own destruction and demise by searching for commitment in so many guys. I gave away my body for a little compromise. I gave in for "I love you's" and shallow compliments that wouldn't satisfy, and at the end of every night there was a bigger emptiness inside. Yes, I knew that it was wrong but I kept suppressing that voice that cried, "don't you realize your body is your pride?!" And every time I cried, I would ask for forgiveness every night thinking that I wasn't worthy in the back of my mind. I felt like a hypocrite apologizing for what I knew I'd do another time. I was tainted with despise, with disgust of my own body and mind. And looking in the mirror I saw how a little girl tried and tried to look for a man to fill the shoes she thought daddy left untied. And while that little girl cried inside, the body of a woman on the outside sacrificed; losing her purity and innocence, still unsatisfied. And while that woman partook in the action of the crime, the little girl inside slowly died and did the time.

But this was my reality, and I'm not embarrassed because I'm the daughter of a pastor or a priest. My only embarrassment comes because I'm the daughter of a King; the only one who was willing to commit for nothing in exchange. All He wanted was for me to be saved, for me to feel loved, to feel a father's embrace, to wipe the tears from my face, and to fill that empty space with security and faith, purity and grace. So I repented and I let Him in my heart one day. He taught me what true love was and the big sacrifice He made.

He began to heal me from the inside-out filling me with inner peace. He began turning my body into the temple that it was always meant to be. And those who knew me then, tell me I'm missing out on good times for outdated beliefs. But they don't know I traded my emptiness for the purity that lives inside me. They don't understand I replaced those lonely nights for a bigger purpose in my life. And they fail to see that I've learned the hard way, how temporary pleasure is just a slow way to die.

And I'm not saying that I'm perfect now because temptations do exist. But God's purpose in me is so loud that the whispers of temptation start to crumble in my midst. And where I once felt I lost my father to the anger that I felt within, God gave him back to me with an extra benefit. Now instead of one dad, I have two; my earthly father and God, my heavenly truth. I thought forever I'd be lost, that no man would come through. But God picked up my broken pieces just to say... I love you.

Trusting in You

Trusting in you, that's the riskiest thing I can do. I've heard it my whole life. Trust is something I once knew. But you see these walls I've built? No one's been able to get through. All I've seen my whole life is people letting me down and making promises they won't keep. But I've realized something; between these walls it's getting lonely. My ways seem to fall short and be unsuccessful only. I said I'd only trust myself but even I have failed me. So if I give You my all, then where's my net of safety?

See, I've only learned to trust what's right in front of me; what is concrete, reasonable, secure, and what is blunt for me. I like my safety, my walls and what is comforting. But stepping out in faith means that my walls will get to crumbling and I have too much pride to let that happen and start humbling.

For too long I've stood without falling inside this comfort zone and I keep reasoning about what it's going to take to step out into the unknown. I just gotta have control. I need to hold on to the steering wheel and I can't let go because all this logic inside me tells me that crashing will be painful and slow.

But my spirit says "No, don't you know that for you to grow, all of your over-logical reasoning must go? You see all these problems that are piling up on you? God is telling you to let them go. He says "for My yoke is easy and My burden is light" and yet instead of letting go, you just keep holding on tight. What do you really have to lose that you haven't already lost? Why don't you just give in and stop trying to fight? You've already proved that your ways still haven't worked at this height, that all of your strength and all your logic don't compare to His might, and that as much as you may think "I can find the answer, I'm a smart guy", God's answers are always going to be just a little more right. And I know you've heard this a million times, but maybe after a million and one you'll actually give faith a try.

So some last words from your spirit, to be a little more blunt about it, I know you TALK a good amount of faith but now it's time to ACT on it."

Another Day Passes

Another day has passed in which I didn't speak to You; in which we shared the same room, the same house and all day You were there waiting but still no words came through. I can only wonder how You have so much patience to deal with my neglect and abuse? With busyness and small errands my time I consume. Then the end of the day comes, finally I remember You. But then sleep overwhelms me before my words get to You.

Why do You stay here day to day with arms open waiting for me to remember Your name? Is it because You know that without You I'd go insane? Is it because You know that without You my life is in vain, that my good works carry no weight and the sun goes away, giving way to clouds and rain? I know it must be frustrating after all the pain, after all the things You went through so that I could be saved. And here I am too busy to speak to You even once a day. So why do You remain? Why is Your love for me so great? I may never understand, for my love is but a grain compared to the expanse of Your love's terrain.

My love is filled with flaws. It's easy to withdraw when things don't go my way; quick and simple to take back when someone makes a mistake. It's not easily displayed. Sometimes my love carries shame, it's tainted, unworthy of the love that You gave. But here You stay, here You wait for the day in which I speak Your name, in which I ask you for forgiveness and give our relationship a second take. And although I'm not worthy You see past my mistakes. You take my hand in Yours and You call me a saint, knowing full well that I'm not worthy of Your grace. And that's why no matter how many times I turn away, You are the one love in this world that I can never replace.

I Cry

Sometimes I cry.
    Yes I
        do cry,
            do sigh,
                do try,
                    do fail,
                        do wish to fly

Like eagles in the sky. But I'm denied, for this world I once called home only butchers all my hopes with lies. Deceived is he who hears but does not open his eyes, for he is blind. He thinks he's high, mightier than life, but fails to realize he does not own what he calls "his" for all is gone the day he dies.

No medicine, nor doctor, nor miracle will suffice, when his day has come no trace of life will bare his eyes. And no good will be his power and might, for all will diminish with that last breath of life.

And so I cry, for he does not know his demise. He claims to know living water, but inside he is dry. In his sorrow he bears no fruit, for in his roots truth does not reside. Obedience does not apply, and in darkness he relies. He puts on his suit and tie ready to face the world a dollar at a time. Yet, his home in ruins lies. With no hope he slowly dies, and without faith in vain is his might.

For in his pain he has turned away, believing that God is the one to blame; that the Redeemer has put him to shame. He blasphemes His name and calls Him the bringer of his pain. See, owning up to responsibilities is not man's forte. For with every bad decision a consequence remains, and though this truth is plain the scapegoat is man's true fame.

So man is no eagle flying mighty in the sky. Far from it in fact, he is the chicken that in his coop lies trembling with fear at the thought of his demise. But wise is he that has opened his eyes. For he is a lamb humble in his ways, a lion that someday will be raised, and an eagle that conquers the sky leading the way. For he dismisses darkness and stands in light, he tramples on death and chooses life.

He will not cry, will not sigh, and will not be afraid to stumble when he tries. He will survive; he will mount on wings like an eagle and fly higher than the man whose pride has knocked him down with all his might. Sometimes he wonders "who am I?" as he falls on his knees to cry because the world has rejected him and pushed him aside. But the day will come when he shall hunger no more neither shall he thirst anymore, for God shall wipe away every tear from his eyes.

Reflection: "I Cry"

This poem addresses the self-sufficient and prideful mentality of mankind. Jesus tells the following parable in Luke 12:16-21:

"The ground of a certain rich man yielded an abundant harvest. He thought to himself, 'What shall I do? I have no place to store my crops.'

"Then he said, 'This is what I'll do. I will tear down my barns and build bigger ones, and there I will store my surplus grain. And I'll say to myself, "You have plenty of grain laid up for many years. Take life easy; eat, drink and be merry."'

"But God said to him, 'You fool! This very night your life will be demanded from you. Then who will get what you have prepared for yourself?'

"This is how it will be with whoever stores up things for themselves but is not rich toward God."

I believe what Jesus was trying to say here is that life is much more than having enough material things. God is the one who provides and satisfies all of our needs. Thus, we do not need to depend solely on ourselves. In fact, God expects us to depend on Him and bring our requests to Him (Philippians 4:6). When we start to believe that we are self-sufficient and we don't need God, that is the beginning of the road to destruction; that is the point in which pride begins to set in. Proverbs 16:8 states that "Pride goes before destruction, a haughty spirit before a fall." You can bank on this. If you believe you are self-sufficient and become prideful, it will not matter how rich you are, you will see destruction. Self-sufficiency also translates into having no fear of the Lord. Anyone who thinks He can do all things by his own power and might demonstrates no fear of God because their self-sufficiency implies that they are somehow greater than God and have no need for Him.

Nevertheless, those who are humble before the Lord are the ones who will be exalted (Luke 14:11). The bible also states in Proverbs 22:4 that "The reward for humility and fear of the Lord is riches and honor and life." If you humble yourself before the Lord and surrender to His will, not only will you be able to fulfill your purpose, but you will be prospered when you do! We surrender to God's will not because He's a tyrant who expects us to do what He wants, but rather because He is a loving Father who truly knows what is best for us and what will bring us happiness, prosperity and satisfaction. So stop trying to be self-sufficient. It's difficult and unnecessary. You have a Father who makes all things work in your favor. Take advantage of the privilege of being called His son/daughter and start seeking His purpose for your life.

The Day I got My Wings

6:55 was this morning's sun rise. So like on many mornings I decided to go outside. I saw the doves flying and thought what a beautiful sight. Then I looked up at Daddy and said, "how come I can't fly?"

"Who told you that ridiculous lie? Just close your eyes and you will see that you can fly, you can reach Me".

So I closed my eyes and waited and waited. Then I waited some more, but nothing happened.

But waiting's outdated. Should I look? I debated. So I peaked at the floor, then I heard Daddy laughing.

He said to me, *"You're not trusting Me. Stop peeking my daughter and you will see that you can fly, you will reach Me".*

So I closed my eyes, but this time tight. And I didn't peak and I didn't fight and I trusted Daddy with all my might. Then all of a sudden I did take flight! I flew and I flew and I took more height!

Then Daddy moved the sun for me, just so that my eyes could see the wings He made so bright for me of every color that I could think. There were even colors unknown to me. And I felt the wind's breath beneath my wings. At that moment I knew, I'd realized something; that spec down there where I awoke this morning looked so faded and temporary. But the sky was immense and never ending. And just when I thought I had seen it all; the sky and the land, the sands of the beach, the flowers all blooming, every and each, I flew a little higher and at my reach was Daddy waiting; waiting for me. And then He spoke that beautiful speech, that language that on earth no one could teach.

But He spoke it to me and I understood. He said, *"Didn't I tell you, that fly you could?"*

But when I tried to reply I couldn't speak, and I felt the warm grass back under my feet; the sun still shining soft, gentle heat. And I opened my eyes only to see, the boy next door staring at me.

So I asked the boy, "Can you fly like me?"

And he said, "no" surprisingly.

I guess he must have lost his wings

    To this sad world's mentality…

Fishes Drowning in Water

LOVE

Is like clean, pure streams of living water; satisfying, refreshing, beautiful to the eye and relaxing to the mind. It is everything divine; the key to the survival of mankind, the thing that revives and brings us back to life.

HUMANS

Are like fishes. We live and thrive off of love. We put nothing else above it. It's a need; a necessary addiction. But it's not all fairytales and fiction. It's beautiful and difficult; easy to fall into but hard to stay in through. But if you stay in long enough your fingers are sure to prune up with the one you love. Funny thing huh? Water is to physical life as love is to the spiritual. It works the same way. It's too bad we seem to have more esteem for the individual and more love for the visual. We lose sight of the original purpose of love until it becomes habitual and no longer meaningful.

We start drowning in it. It's no longer clean but tainted. It doesn't take long for us to get acquainted before we start falling in love. Although it's more like we faint in. Then we wake up and realize it wasn't true love. So maybe we faked it? Then we end up crying, "Why does love hurt? We hate it!"

People die for love, but not like they use to. They no longer risk their lives for the one they love. Now they commit suicide over rejected love, or threaten to take their own lives if their "love" won't come. We seem to put obsession in the place of love. I have to wonder how this all looks from above?

I wonder how God looks at His sons and daughters as His intention for love with our actions we slaughter. Can't help but think…

We must look a lot like fishes drowning in water.

Reflection: "Fishes Drowning in Water"

In this poem I compare humans to fish and love to water. The point I'm trying to make is that sometimes love, which is supposed to be something we thrive off of, becomes a dangerous thing. Love can easily be confused with infatuation and can also easily turn into obsession. What I'm getting at is that if fishes aren't supposed to drown in water which is their life source, we as humans should not be drowning in love, which is ultimately what keeps us alive. The bible teaches us that God is love (1 John 4:16). God is also our source of life (John 5:26). Therefore, love is our source of life. Hence, we should not be drowning in love but thriving in it.

Nevertheless, due to the misuse of love, many people have come to believe that love no longer truly exists. Thus, we see more and more divorces at early stages in marriages and we rarely see people growing old together like they use to. We don't "stay in long enough" to see our significant other grow old with us. We've tainted love with false expectations and we've failed to be realistic. I think we've forgotten the "in sickness and health", "for richer or for poorer" and "'til death do us part" pieces of the wedding vows. Why is that?

If God is a God of love and we are His creations, why have we forgotten how to love? "Love your neighbor as yourself" (Mark 12:31). That's the second greatest commandment after loving God above all things. "Husbands, love your wives, just as Christ loved the church and gave Himself up for her" (Ephesians 5:25). The bible teaches that love is about sacrificing ourselves for others. It's not about fulfilling our own selfish desires. And you might say "well if I'm being treated badly I need to be a little selfish to get what I deserve". However, if you're being treated badly it's just best to leave the situation altogether. But my point is, if none of us were selfish, then none of us would be treated badly because we would all be willing to sacrifice for each other. Am I being unrealistic? It may seem that way, but being selfish only contributes to the problem and it in no way deters it. I believe unselfish love does still exist. I encourage you to take part in that kind of love. Love was made for us, just like water was made for fishes. We've just got to learn to swim a little better with each other.

My Biggest Enemy

It seems every time you look at me there's a hint of hatred in your eyes; a distinct nature of despise, just a glimpse of anger in disguise. I just have to wonder why? A part of me knows but a part of me just wants to cry and ask a million questions. But I'm silenced by my own sighs because I think I know why.

And see I know what you're thinking because I've thought it in my mind: where am I going? What am I doing? And who am I? It seems the answer is clear but my faith withers when faced with the reality of this life. I'm trying to live one day at a time but the days disperse into seconds gone by. I try to be wise and say all the right lines but I'm far from that perfect woman I've visualized. Yet, you torture me with those eyes, pointing out my indiscretions, causing this repetition of guilt in my mind. I wind and rewind my own faults all the time. But it's you who reminds and puts the blindfold to my eyes, you take away my sight so that I can be blind to the good that's hidden within me inside.

Yea it seems you're my biggest enemy. You're the one I can't leave behind; the one who brings me down, who won't let me live my life, the one who is there to point out every lie, who tells me to close my lips when I should speak my mind, who brings me back down when I'm feeling so high. Yes, you're my biggest enemy. But you're my secret, all mine. And though I wish I'd let you go someday, you still follow behind.

You're name I won't mention because no one should know, but every time I look in the mirror, I just can't let you go.

Reflection: "My Biggest Enemy"

Hopefully you understood that the biggest enemy I was talking about in this poem was myself. I feel like we all struggle with ourselves sometimes. I know that I am my biggest critic. It's easy to judge ourselves and be hard on ourselves when we make mistakes. Yet, we have to realize that even when we make mistakes, God who is perfect, is willing to forgive us. The question is: why aren't we willing to forgive ourselves? Why do we look in the mirror and think the worst of ourselves sometimes?

So maybe you aren't where you want to be in life. Maybe you're not sure of who you are or what your purpose is. But the answer to all of that is found in God. God is the one who created you and so He is the one who can tell you what your purpose is. The more you build your relationship with God, the more you will get to know Him and the more He can reveal to you about your purpose.

In terms of not being where you want to be, just remember that God does have a plan for your life and that "He who started the good work in you, will carry it on to completion" (Philippians 1:6). So you don't need to worry about wasted time. Be proactive today, do something about it now. Chances are that God has placed a passion or a gift in you, so pursue it! Wherever your passion is, there your purpose also lies and your prosperity awaits. So if you feel like you aren't where you want to be, start planning your next step. Give yourself a deadline and start working towards that goal that you have in mind. It doesn't matter how old you are. It's never too late to start living a purpose-driven life in God.

The Desire to Forget

Tears are running down my cheeks.

And here I hide thinking no one sees.

But You oh God see my pain.

You understand my fears.

Just wish there was a way to get away from here,

To get away from me and not have to feel what I feel.

I made a mistake; I know I've got to wait to heal.

Went down the road I didn't have to take

And now I feel like I'm lost in a field.

Why me? I ask myself

As my words get caught in my throat. I'm asking for help.

I don't want to feel what I feel for him.

Just wish it would all go away.

Just want to forget the "I love you's", the embraces, his face.

I just want to erase it all away.

Pretend it never happened; forget I ever looked at him.

I just want to get away.

I just want to get away.

Reflection: "The Desire to Forget"

Heartbreak…This is something we all go through. It's very easy to get carried away and want to forget everything. It would be simple to leave to some far off place and pretend it never happened. But the fact of the matter is that even if you could get away, the feelings of hurt would follow you wherever you go. But one thing we do know is that with the help of God, time can heal all wounds. The bible says in Psalm 34:18-19 that "the LORD is close to the brokenhearted and saves those who are crushed in spirit. The righteous person may have many troubles, but the LORD delivers him from them all". Although heartbreak is painful, how beautiful it is to know that in our time of most desperate need God is close to us and He delivers us from all our troubles and pain. Psalm 147:3 also says that "God heals the broken hearted and binds up their wounds." That means that God is the remedy for your broken heart.

I also know that loneliness is a side effect of heart break. But God says "fear not for I am with you; be not dismayed, for I am your God; I will strengthen you, I will help you, I will uphold you with my righteous right hand" (Isaiah 41:10). Break ups make us feel helpless, weak, and even destroyed. Yet, God is with us to be our strength, to be our help and to be our healer. He is the one who tends to your broken heart. He will never leave you or forsake you in your time of most need (Deuteronomy 31:6). He will be your sufficiency. 2 Corinthians 12:10 says, "when I am weak, then I am strong". In our time of weakness we need to still rejoice knowing that God not only gives us the strength we need, but He IS the strength we need to carry on (Habakkuk 3:19). In our time of weakness we become strong because God becomes our sufficiency and fills any emptiness that is inside us. If you are dealing with heartbreak today, let God be your strength and sufficiency and believe that He can and will heal your heart. You don't have to feel alone, God is with you at all times.

He's with you at all times because He has taken a special interest in you. 1 John 3:1 states "See what kind of love the Father has given to us that we should be called children of God; and so we are." We are children of God and He loves us like a father loves a child. Sometimes God allows the heartbreak to happen because it is simply not His will for us to be with that person. I am not implying that God is some kind of tyrant that doesn't want us to be with the person we want to be with. However, I am saying that just like our earthly fathers care about who we date, get upset when we are heartbroken and have an urge to protect us from harm, God also wants to protect us and care for us in that way. The only difference is that God is omnipotent which means He is all-knowing. Since He is all-knowing, He knows exactly who is going to make us happy, and who is going to walk with us and help us fulfill the purpose He has placed in our lives. So don't worry if it didn't work out with that person. Better **will** come.

Take this opportunity to reevaluate yourself; to improve any area of your life that needs improvement and to seek God more passionately. Remember that when we delight ourselves in the Lord, He will give us the desires of our hearts. So take this as an opportunity. Don't look at it as a loss of someone. Look at it as finding yourself. It's not the end of the world even if it feels like it. I know what it's like to stand in those shoes, but just know that God is standing right next to you ready to take you by the hand and keep moving forward with you! He loves you and He most certainly isn't going to abandon you now.

You Know Me Best

I will not fall asunder. My strength is in you oh God. You cover me with Your hand. Your voice calls out to me like thunder. You are my rod and my staff; the one who makes me indestructible. This seed will not rebel; I'm incorruptible. I will not be broken down by the situation at hand. I stand, knowing exactly who I am; a daughter of God, determined and unwavering. I follow through with God's plans.

No more tears will I cry though I walk through desert sands. Though my own plans slip through my hands, I will not fear, I will not doubt and I will not rebel. I'm done with being the generic brand of a Christian that comes preserved in jars and cans. I must be different, fresh fruit is what I'll be; an aroma desirable to my king. I'll be the exception, the anomaly, predestined to be an abnormality because an explosion is what I'm bound to be. I have to be exactly what my God requires of me. My destiny, what's driving me is God's fire inside of me.

And I refuse to bow down. I refuse to fall down. I refuse to take smiles and replace them with frowns. See my goal is heaven-bound. So my head I will raise, it's not facing the ground. The circumstance may be hard, but my spirit's on guard.

And I will give glory to my God regardless of how things are. He will be sanctified in every situation because He will withhold me with His arm. Holy is the King who took scars to keep me out of harm. How can I be angry? How can I be upset when God watches over all my best interests? I will trust in You oh Lord and forget all the rest because at the end of the day, only You know me best.

Meant for More

I'm tired of listening to all this negativity around me, tired of witnessing death and violence surround me, tired of the hopelessness, tired of the laziness, tired of people telling me simply "you're not making it". There's nothing simple or normal about a generation degenerating, disintegrating, fading into the background of life and reciprocating the same anger and negative strife because they've become hopeless and lost their purpose. Never being told they were meant for more than this and so they fall through the cracks of life into the abyss.

But who stands up to the plate and puts an end to this? Who says enough is enough and decides to make a difference? What happened to that mentality that we could achieve anything? That we could be anything? I refuse to believe this was just a notion of the past because I won't stand to watch this generation fail because you couldn't see your purpose past the stereotypes and laughs. See you were meant for more; meant to stand out but not meant to be the outcast, meant to follow great ideas but never meant to be last because you're the solution, you're the future not the past.

So I don't care if someone told you that you can't because you can. I don't care if someone told you that you won't amount to anything in life because you will. Don't just accept defeat and stand still. Find your purpose, find your talent, find that skill, become someone great and let your dreams become real, because life is for the living, but you've got to LIVE your life. You can't just spend your time sitting around waiting for things to drop out of the sky. There's greatness in you! Take a look in your eyes. You were meant for more than this, you need to realize!

So stop looking at yourself through the eyes of another's judgments and condemnations. Stop living your life like the statistic that people have made you. Be someone, do something, but don't let the world fade you because you were meant for more than this, you are not worthless. You were meant for more than this, you are not hopeless. You were meant for more than this, so go and work your purpose.

Leave the Past behind You

Why are you so focused on your past? You're obsessing over memories that were meant to fade and not last, remembering things that only make you sad; things that only make you mad and that only make you question why. Why, when I didn't make you for that? You see I exist outside of time. I'm the Beginning and the End. But I've limited you to this chronos. Have you ever asked yourself what's the message I'm trying to send?

I made time only move forward for you. There's no rewind or pause. Too many of you would be stuck in the past, stuck in moments that weren't meant to last. You'd never move forward. You'd be stunted, trapped behind a glass wall, always in the middle of a fall, never quite landing at all. But see, if you had never fallen, I couldn't have picked you up. Yet, you keep obsessing over your fall, zooming in close ups, while forgetting that in that time of your life you were drinking from a death cup. You focus on these mistakes of yours, as if everyone around you knew exactly where it is you struck

Out. But I'm here to pull you in. Don't you realize your past ceased to exist the day I spoke the words "it is finished". And by finished I meant done, as in you don't have to keep reliving your failures one by one. Because while you wallowed away in sin spending your heavenly inheritance, I received you back, forgetting your past, prodigal son. See your battle's already been won. So you don't need to keep fighting the past I defeated for you on that cross. You don't have to carry the burden of your sins on your back like a punishment. I know it weighs a ton because I already carried it once. And once was enough, so when will you give it up?

Stop pulling chains that have already been broken. Stop looking for "I love you's" that I've already spoken. Stop searching for a purpose that's standing right before you; not in your past but in your present because I'm your token. I'm your way out. I'm the purpose for which you're searching. I'm the one who can fill that void that you keep trying to fill with person after person. Aren't you tired of filling yourself with temporary fixes that only trick your mind into thinking you're no longer conflicted? While deep down inside you know your past keeps inflicting these memories that keep you trapped and afflicted, with habits and burdens you haven't quite kicked yet. You're living your life walking in circles around your past. Guess it hasn't quite clicked yet that I'm that permanent fix you've been avoiding.

The one you keep ignoring. The one you called outdated and boring. The one who you said is probably just an old bible story. The one you've claimed doesn't hear you when you call begging and imploring. But I'm here today and my heart I'm pouring. Your purpose wasn't to live in vain but to mount on wings like an eagle; you should be soaring. Because I'm the one who stands next to you holding you up when against you the world is warring. And like a lion I defend you with everything I've got; hear me roaring. I won't let the mistakes of your past bring you down; it's your heart I'm restoring. So forget about your yesterday, don't you realize my mercy for you is made new every morning? Oh what I wouldn't do for thee if you'd only dare to speak my name and adore me. Here I am standing at your door and I knock, will you hear my voice and open up for me?

Or will you once again ignore me? Reverting back to your past, to those moments that for so long have kept you trapped. Let me be your hero, I promise I won't put you through that. But you have to let go. I need you to forgive and take my hand at last because I'm your future and to be with Me you can't live in the past. I want so much more for you. Just give Me your burdens is all I ask. Let Me love you with a love that's unsurpassed, with a love that's so vast, it never ceases to exist, never fails, it always lasts. Let me show you how much I love you. You're a new creation in my eyes; without blemish, without wrinkle. You were predestined to be mine. It's your destiny to shine. But if you want to be connected to this vine, then you've got to leave your past behind.

What If?

What if there really are no limits? What if impossible really doesn't exist? What if we used words to solve problems and not our fists? What if we learned to look at others past their outer image? What if every breath we took really did make a difference? What if all our mistakes could be unwritten? What if happiness wasn't forbidden? What if we really are forgiven? What if life isn't just this? What if there's more than we ever imagined? What if we all really did have a purpose? What if life really wasn't hopeless?

What if every time someone told you that you couldn't, you actually could? What if when they bet you, you wouldn't, you actually would? What if everything made sense and you finally understood? What if you tried the foods you hate and found that they were actually good? What if one day it starts to rain and you don't put on your hood? What if you let the rain embrace you and soak you where you stood? What if those thoughts you're always thinking were actually a book? What if life wasn't about being safe? What if a risk you took? What if you looked in the direction that you never thought to look?

What if you looked at yourself in the mirror and thought you were amazing? What if you found that life was more than the problems that you're facing? What if we made good use of time and decided to prevent the lazy? What if we really started trusting God and were genuinely praising? What if for once you did believe in all those dreams you talk about chasing? What if some day is just today, disguised in the lie of too far away? And what if you fought the urge to escape and just decided to stay? What if you stood your ground and took on whatever came your way? What if nothing could bring you down at the end of the day? What if you are meant to be happy but you're standing in your own way?

What if? What if?

What if you stopped asking yourself what if, and actually did? What if you actually followed that vision that you almost missed? Or achieved the goal you were so close to that you almost kissed? What if you actually accomplished all those things on your mental list?

       What if…

         What if…

           You just decided to live?

Final Remarks

I pray that this book has been a blessing for your life and that it has encouraged you to seek out the purpose God has for you. However, before you can seek that purpose it is important to establish a relationship with God. The first step to beginning that relationship is receiving Jesus Christ as your Lord and Savior. If you have not yet accepted Him, I can tell you that it is the most important decision of your life.

John 3:16 teaches that "God so loved the world that He gave His only begotten son so that whoever believes in Him, will not perish but have eternal life."

The fact of the matter is that we are all sinners and we all fall short of the glory of God (Romans 3:23). No one can say that they have not sinned. Sin is simply doing something that is not pleasing to God. We all make mistakes. We are not perfect. Because of our sins, we were supposed to be sentenced to death, meaning that we would not inherit eternal life after our human life. The bible states that the wages (the pay we deserve/ the consequence) for sin is death. Yet, the good news is that when Jesus died on the cross He redeemed us of our sins. He paid a price that we were supposed to pay. He paid it with His death. He remained dead for three days and then resurrected on the third day. Because of that sacrifice and resurrection, we now have eternal life and access to the Father and we are able to build a close and personal relationship with Him (Ephesians 3:12). But it all begins with one decision.

The bible teaches us what is necessary to be saved in Romans 10:9-13: "If you declare with your mouth, "Jesus is Lord," and believe in your heart that God raised Him from the dead, you will be saved. For it is with your heart that you believe and are justified, and it is with your mouth that you profess your faith and are saved. As Scripture says, "Anyone who believes in Him will never be put to shame." For there is no difference between Jew and Gentile—the same Lord is Lord of all and richly blesses all who call on Him, for, "Everyone who calls on the name of the Lord will be saved."

It is as simple as believing and confessing. If you're tired of your old lifestyle and tired of all the burdens in your life, I want to present to you a God who loves you, who restores you and who wants to be your Father and best friend. Let Him restore your life and help you carry those burdens. What do you have to lose? If you are ready to make the biggest decision of your life I ask you to read aloud the following prayer:

Dear God in heaven, I come to you in the name of Jesus. I acknowledge that I am a sinner, and I am sorry for my sins and the life that I have lived; I need your forgiveness.

I believe that your only begotten son Jesus Christ shed His precious blood on the cross at Calvary and died for my sins, and I am now willing to turn away from my sin.

You said in Your Holy Word, Romans 10:9 that if we confess the Lord our God and believe in our hearts that God raised Jesus from the dead we would be saved.

Right now I confess Jesus as the Lord of my soul. With my heart, I believe that God raised Jesus from the dead. This very moment I accept Jesus Christ as my own personal Savior and according to His Word, right now I am saved.

Thank you, Jesus for your unlimited grace which has saved me from my sins. I thank you Jesus that your grace never leads to license, but rather it always leads to repentance. Therefore Lord Jesus, transform my life so that I may bring glory and honor to you alone and not to myself. Thank you, Jesus for dying for me and giving me eternal life. Amen.

Prayer adapted from:

http://www.salvationprayer.info/prayer.html

If you've repeated this prayer, then I congratulate you on making the best decision of your life. You have taken a great step in establishing a relationship with the one true God. Now you can begin your journey to seeking and intentionally fulfilling the purpose God has predestined for your life.

My hope is that this book has empowered you, regardless of what gender you may be, to become a man or woman that lives a life intentionally trying to fulfill your purpose. Whether it be on a small scale by treating people with kindness, respect and love, or whether it be by taking a stand for God by sticking to your morals and values even if they go against the norm of society, I pray that you choose to be different. The bible says the following in 1 Peter 2:9:

"But you are a chosen race, a royal priesthood, a holy nation, a people for His own possession, that you may proclaim the excellencies of him who called you out of darkness into his marvelous light."

We were separated by God and He has called us out of darkness and into His light. He has called us to be part of His holy nation so that we can proclaim His message of salvation, forgiveness and love to the world. That is our ultimate purpose. It can be carried out in many ways. God has given each of us different gifts and talents. These gifts were no coincidence. God wants us to intentionally use the tools He has given us in order to accomplish the goal of spreading the gospel to a world that is in desperate need of the message of Christ. So today I make a call for you to be bold for Christ and to use whatever opportunities and gifts God has placed in your life to do something great for God.

Now, doing something great may sound intimidating to some people. It's easy to feel like we are not adequate enough to accomplish the tasks God has asked us to do. But let me remind you that God turned a shepherd boy into a King when He chose David. He turned a man with a stuttering problem into a messenger that would go before the Pharaoh of Egypt bearing the message, "Let my people go", when He chose Moses. This is the same God who rose up a woman named Esther, (whose name meant "hidden") to stand before a King with the threat of being killed, in order to save her people from execution. Through the most unlikely people, God has manifested His glory and has proven just how great He is.

So please, don't underestimate God's ability to make something great out of something small because it's not about what YOU can do. It's about what God can do THROUGH you. God has a greater purpose to accomplish with this world and you and I are a part of it. The only question left to answer is: are you willing to let Him use you as an instrument to fulfill that purpose? I hope the answer to that question is yes and I pray that from this day forward you will begin to live your life with purpose on purpose.

For My Godson: Jaydyn

On June 26th a new star was introduced into this world, shining a light upon those who welcomed him reminding them that hope is something still worth being explored.

He's an answer to prayers reminding us that God has heard. That even in the midst of our hurt God gives us strength greater than we could've asked for. And this star's entrance was of high eminence, allowing us to witness the evidence that the best things in life are worth waiting for.

So my prayer for this little star, for this little ray of light is that you may walk in the ways of the Lord all your life; that you may never have to face unnecessary strife. That you will bring joy and laughter into the lives of many and that your words will be more powerful than the words of those that came before you. That you will be an inspiration and an example to others. That you will be blessed with all blessings and bring much joy to your father and mother.

I pray that you be successful in whatever you choose, and that you enjoy the feeling of being your own person and walking in your own shoes. But mostly I pray that when you embark on your journey and take your ride through life's cruise, that I'll always be there to witness all the wonderful things life has in store for you.

Spanish Preview

El Que Te Espera

Yo se que nadie se ha dado cuenta de que sufres. Que tu almohada ha recogido mas lagrimas de lo que quieres admitir. Que aunque te llenes de tristeza por dentro todavía puedes sonreír. Que te pones una máscara de felicidad para cubrir todo ese dolor que llevas guardando por dentro. Pero algo te tengo que decir y hablo a tu corazón, hablo a tu centro. Yo no te hice con tristeza, ni con dolor o resentimiento. Más te hice con amor y gozo, si es Mi Espíritu que llevas por dentro. Quizás piensas que nadie te amara, que nadie piensa en ti, y que no les importaras.

Sin embargo, mis pensamientos por ti son como la arena del mar, que no se pueden contar. Si es que te he estado pensando desde antes de la creación de este mundo. ¿No te das cuenta que el amor que te tengo es profundo? Que cuando nadie está a tu lado soy Yo quien te cubro, soy Yo que te escucho y soy Yo tu escudo. Soy Yo el que pelea por ti, el que levanta bandera, Jehová Nissi, si clamas a mí al instante te responderé. Me levantare a defenderte a ti porque eres lo más que amo y todavía cuenta no te has dado.

¿Es que acaso no ves lo que Yo veo? ¿Qué hay grandeza en ti? ¿Que Yo no te llame para que fueras reflexión de ti si no de Mi? Que te hice perfectamente, semilla incorruptible, indestructible. No te cree para este mundo y por eso algunas veces te sientes incompatible. Pero no te me pongas sensible. ¿No te das cuenta que por ti hice lo que para cualquier otro hombre fue imposible? Por ti Yo di mi vida. Fui Yo que pague tu precio, porque nadie más en esta tierra se atrevió a pasar por ese sufrimiento. Lo hice por amor y de eso no me arrepiento. ¿Es que no te has dado cuenta que tu y Yo somos la historia de amor más perfecta? Que todo lo que hice fue solo para poder amarte por una vida eterna. Es que es Mi nombre que está marcado en tu corazón, es Mi Espíritu que esta aferrado a tu alma, es Mi aliento de vida que sale de ti cuando respiras y es Mi imagen que ves en el espejo cuando te miras.

Soy Yo quien ha estado contigo. Soy Yo el que te ha dado consuelo y lo único que espero es que me dejes restaurar tu mundo entero. Porque todavía te sigo amando, eres tu el que he separado y eres tu al que sigo esperando. Así que te propongo algo… si quieres una vida eterna conmigo te prometo que te amare por los siglos de los siglos. Pero la decisión es tuya. Yo no te obligare. ¿Me aceptaras o me rechazaras? Pacientemente te esperare pero recuerda que muy pronto… Yo regresare.

Sinceramente,

El Verdadero Amor de tu Vida,

El que te espera, El que te cuida, y El que nunca te olvida.

Firme Estaré

Es un dolor fuerte que late muy adentro de mi pecho. Mi corazón está llorando, esta desecho. Solo esperando acabar con el tormento. Mi condición de mujer intento defender mientras siento este nudo que se acumula en mi pecho con la punta de mis dedos. Es la razón de mi tensión, no lo puedo describir como depresión, si es lamento lo que añoro en esta condición. Y mientras mis días se van borrando, siento que sin una contestación, en vano sigo orando.

Esta enfermedad es tan absurda que hasta mi vida he dejado de vivir. Solo mi vergüenza cubre esta tristeza que llevo dentro de mí cuando la gente mira a este pájaro sin alas en cual me convertí. Me he sentido humillada ante mi reflexión. Siento que las paredes se caen en destrucción. Sin firmeza habla mi voz y cuando ando en la calle solo tropiezo. No soy la misma de antes. No soy la mujer con alta auto estima que se ríe de mí en las fotos. Esa mujer que un día ardía con pasión para la vida ya no existe y solo quedan cenizas. Una mujer que antes parecía no poder ser derribada, pero ahora "por favor llévense esta maldición de mi!" es lo que grita mi alma. Pero solo el silencio me respondió y me enfrió por dentro sin nadie que me derrita. En amargura me derrumbo, pero siento que algo persiste en mi corazón.

Si, ay algo que persiste y es más fuerte que yo. Algo que había olvidado por tanto tiempo. Como canción de esperanza dentro de mi disfrazado, empiezan a salir palabras de mis labios. Ya no lo puedo aguantar, y me empiezan a bajar las lágrimas. Y mi fe me rescata de mi misma. Era lo que siempre me hacía falta. Pero me dicen que estoy mal, que los milagros no existen. Pero ahora sé que soy fuerte, porque mi fe es la que me dirige. Porque los doctores no han conocido a el Dios que yo sirvo, que ha escuchado mis oraciones y cada palabra que yo digo. Así que con todas mis fuerzas resistiré, y al que me pregunta le contestare, que firme estaré sabiendo que El es Dios, mi Redentor, mi Sanador, El que vive hoy, mañana y por los siglos de los siglos.

Latido del Corazón

Oí su corazón latir una vez,
Pero eso fue hace muchos días.
En ese tiempo en cual no sabía, las miserias que la vida me traería.
Antes de que mis sueños y los misterios de la vida se enfriarían.
Tan fríos como el abismo de mi alma.
Un vacio…

Es lo que se forma cuando decisiones son tomadas, sin medir las consecuencias. La amargura crece, y la vida se desenvuelve.

No es bonito como lo hacen sonar, la temprana edad más decisiones mal tomadas solo me trajeron responsabilidades que no estaba lista para enfrentar. La expectativa de ajustarme al molde de una madre responsable por la vida de otro ser era una carga más allá del control que yo pensaba tener. Pero la realidad me alcanzo cuando en mi vientre lo vi creciendo. No era lo suficiente mayor, lo suficiente sabia, ni madura para saberlo, pero de mi vientre el me gritaba, rogándome, "!NO, MAMA NO LO HAGAS!"

Y ahora me pregunto, ¿y si no lo hubiese hecho, que hubiera sido de ese hijo? Si no me hubiese sometido a las peleas y argumentos. Mis padres pensaban que gravemente me había equivocado y el padre del niño se negaba a tomar responsabilidad por su parte del trato, ¿pero que hubiese pasado si no hubiese renunciado a ese hijo tan sagrado?

Aunque todos los "quizás" no significan mucho ya. Si lo que antes crecía en mí, ya en el polvo está enterrado. Y puedo sentir su aliento de infante con cada soplo de viento que hace. Puedo sentir sus lágrimas amargas en mi boca con cada gota de agua que del cielo brota. Podría jurar que lo escuche decir mi nombre desde mi vientre, llorando y suplicando en desconfianza. El sabe que lo escuche, y que lo mande a callarse, y que por mi interés su vida le quite, llevándome también su confianza de bebe.

Y yo se que él lo sabe, el sabe la verdad, que yo si escuche su corazón palpitar.

Reflexión: "Latido del Corazón"

Este poema no fue escrito con la intención de juzgar a ninguna mujer que haya tenido un aborto. De hecho escribí el poema en primera persona por esta razón. No estoy tratando de ofenderla si usted ha tenido un aborto. Sé que el aborto no es una decisión fácil y que puede causar una pesada carga de culpa después. No existe una manera bonita de decir esto; el aborto no es agradable a los ojos de Dios. Sin embargo, después de que se hace, ya está hecho y no hay nada que puedas hacer al respecto en ese momento. Pero Dios no quiere que vivas con la carga de esa culpa para siempre. Parte de la carga de nuestro pecado es la culpa. Cuando cometemos un crimen contra Dios, estamos agobiados con la culpa del pecado. El propósito de la culpa es para hacernos saber cuándo hemos hecho algo mal. Sin embargo, cuando Jesús murió en la cruz, no sólo llevo la carga de su pecado, sino también la carga de su culpa. Si de verdad se arrepiente de sus pecados, Dios es clemente y misericordioso para perdonar y tomar la carga de su culpa. Una vez que Dios nos perdona, nosotros ya no tenemos que sentirnos culpables. Debemos darnos cuenta de que si Dios es santo, perfecto, omnipotente y poderoso, y Él es capaz de perdonarnos, entonces debemos también perdonarnos a nosotros mismos.

Esta parte siguiente no se aplica a todas las mujeres que han tenido abortos, ya que hay muchas razones que las mujeres tienen abortos. Sin embargo, si el embarazo no deseado que resultó en aborto se produjo porque la mujer era sexualmente activa sin estar casada, entonces debemos encontrar una manera de evitar que esto vuelva a suceder en el futuro. La respuesta es la pureza. Me doy cuenta que el mundo nos ha convencido que el sexo fuera del matrimonio es la norma. Pero los estándares de Dios son más altos que aquellos del mundo. 1 Corintios 6:19-20 dice, "¿O ignoráis que vuestro cuerpo es templo del Espíritu Santo, el cual está en vosotros, el cual tenéis de Dios, y que no sois vuestros? Porque habéis sido comprados por precio; glorificad, pues, a Dios en vuestro cuerpo y en vuestro espíritu, los cuales son de Dios". La Biblia nos enseña que nuestros cuerpos fueron comprados por Jesucristo cuando Él murió en la cruz. Nosotros pertenecemos a Dios y debemos honrarlo con nuestros cuerpos. Tú eres especial para Dios, y Él quiere que usted sólo le de su cuerpo al hombre que Él ha escogido como su pareja perfecta. Dios quiere que permanezcamos puras para nuestro propio beneficio. Para que no se produzcan cosas como los embarazos no deseados. Él quiere que vivamos una vida plena y feliz pero también quiere que nosotros vivimos nuestras vidas en el orden correcto. Tú eres su hija y como cualquier padre amoroso, Él quiere lo mejor para sus hijas. Déjalo entrar en tu corazón, y deja que te enseñe lo que es el verdadero amor. Nunca es demasiado tarde.

Que Significa Ser Un Padre

Cualquier persona puede llamarse padre, pero solo a un hombre verdadero se le dice papa.

Ser un papa significa,

Ser recibido en la puerta por tus hijos gritando "Papi!!"

Ser un papa significa siempre guardar la imagen de tus hijos como si todavía fueran pequeñitos.

Ser un papa significa velar como lo que Dios puso en tus manos crece y se desenvuelve.

Ser un papa significa una responsabilidad que nunca se envejece.

Pero papi, ser mi papa significa que a ser parte de mi vida te decidiste.

Ser mi papa significa que me amas aunque a veces patalee y grite.

Ser mi papa quiere decir corriendo conmigo al CVS porque ya es ese tiempo del mes.

Ser mi papa significa que me diste un abrazo cuando más lo necesite.

Ser mi papa significa recibiendo un mensaje temprano en la mañana diciendo papi ora por mí que voy a coger mis exámenes.

Ser mi papa significa llegando a mis graduaciones para ver me cumplir otra meta.

Ser mi papa significa siempre diciendo lo preciso para hacer me sonreír.

Ser mi papa significa editando mis poemas aunque ya tienes tanto que hacer.

Ser mi papa significa siempre creyendo en mi y ensenándome a tener fe.

Ser mi papa significa que eres el ejemplo del amor de Dios todos los días.

Ser mi papa significa que no hay otro hombre que te pueda reemplazar en mi vida.

ABOUT THE AUTHOR

Sasha Enid Medina was born in Hartford, Connecticut on November 27th, 1990. She is currently working on a bachelor's degree in English at the University of Saint Joseph in West Hartford, CT. She is actively involved with the youth in the Connecticut area. Sasha currently serves as a Leadership Mentor at the University of Saint Joseph as well as a youth leader at International Churches Development Christian Ministry. Besides writing poetry, Sasha also worships God through her Spoken Word ministry, SEM (*Speak Empower Motivate*) Ministry. Sasha can be contacted through various social networks including Facebook, Twitter, YouTube and Tumblr.

Facebook: www.facebook.com/SashaE.Medina
Twitter: www.twitter.com/Sasha_Medina
YouTube: www.youtube.com/SashaEnid27
Tumblr: www.sashaenid27.tumblr.com

Sources

"Pornography Statistics." *Family Safe Media*. Nextphase, Inc. d.b.a., n.d. Web. 6 Sep 2013. <http://familysafemedia.com/pornography_statistics.html>.

"Prayer of Salvation." *Salvation Prayer*. Salvationprayer.info, n.d. Web. 6 Sep 2013. <http://www.salvationprayer.info/prayer.html>.

59970415R00077

Made in the USA
Middletown, DE
14 August 2019